# The Books of Catullus

GAIUS VALERIUS CATULLUS was bor
in 84 BCE and died in Rome in 54 BCE. 1          ...is life
survives. What is known is inferred from th          or from indirect
secondary sources. He was a contemporary of Cicero and Caesar,
the latter a friend of his father, and an immediate antecedent of the
Augustan poets Horace, Propertius and Ovid. His surviving poems
are among the finest lyric verse of ancient Rome.

SIMON SMITH has published five collections of poetry. His third
collection, *Mercury* (Salt), was long-listed for the Costa Prize in
2007. A selected poems, *More Flowers Than You Could Possibly Carry*,
appeared from Shearsman in 2016, and his latest pamphlet is *Salon
Noir* (Equipage, 2016). He is Reader in Creative Writing at the
University of Kent, was a Hawthornden Writing Fellow in 2009,
and a judge of the National Poetry Prize in 2004. He holds a PhD
from the University of Glasgow.

# the books of
# CATULLUS

*translated and edited*

*by*

Simon Smith

**Carcanet Classics**

First published in Great Britain in 2018 by

CARCANET PRESS
Alliance House, 30 Cross Street
Manchester M2 7AQ
www.carcanet.co.uk

Translation, selection, and editorial matter
© Simon Smith, 2018

Title-page artwork: Felicity Allen, *Crowned Poet: a drawing of
the puppet made by Paul Klee, 1919* (2012). Original in colour.
Book Design: Luke Allan

A CIP catalogue record for this book is available from
the British Library, ISBN 9781784105501

The publisher acknowledges financial assistance
from Arts Council England

# Contents

*to the teachers,*
*particularly Reg Nash for the Latin*
*and Olive Burnside for the poetry*

# Introduction

Catullus is one of the most popular and most translated Latin poets. His popularity continues to grow, with the variety of translations proliferating and accelerating since the 1960s. The dates of his birth and death are uncertain; according to St Jerome, Gaius Valerius Catullus was born in Verona in 87 BCE and died in Rome in 57 BCE. However, evidence from the poems shows that he was still alive as late as 54 BCE: Poem 11 alludes to Julius Caesar's invasion of Britain. Mention of the soldier and politician in a scattering of poems make it clear Catullus was living at the time of Caesar (apparently a friend of his father's) and other Roman notables, who walk into (and then out of) the poems, such as Cicero. He was on the staff of Memmius in the province of Bithynia in 57 (Poem 10), and knew contemporary Roman poets and writers such as Cornelius Nepos, the dedicatee of the poems (Poem 1). The identification of his lover, the noblewoman Clodia Metelli, named 'Lesbia' in the poems, is not a certainty, although likely. In addition, the text shows the poet was familiar with, and translated versions of, the Greek and Hellenic poets Sappho and Callimachus. These facts, and others gleaned from the poems and corroborated by secondary sources, are as much as we can be certain of.

Despite the scarcity of facts about Catullus's life, there is enough circumstantial evidence, wider historical record and textual allusion to build a biographical interpretation of the poems. Indeed, Daisy Dunn's *Catullus' Bedspread: The Life of Rome's Most Erotic Poet* is full-blown biography, proving that this approach to Catullus and his poems, which perpetuates his reputation as Latin literature's most popular and accessible poet, can yield a fast-paced read. Fictional accounts of Catullus's life and times are not unheard of either, nor are they particularly new: Thornton Wilder's epistolary novel *The Ides of March*, dating from 1948, is a minor masterpiece in its own right.

The biographical approach to Catullus is so attractive because of, rather than despite, the limited factual evidence. What facts we do have (very few), combined with scraps of suggestive hearsay (rather more), amount to a partial account with enough scope for creative interpolation that a convincing and absorbing story is easily constructed. Such accounts recover Catullus from anonymity and obscurity (the resting place of most Latin poets) and make of him an apparently red-blooded, three-dimensional protagonist.

This attraction to biography does not rise plainly and simply from the salacious content of the poems, but equally from their seeming intimacy, the way they address the reader personally. For example, Poem 8 – the first poem this translator attempted – positions the reader as if looking through a keyhole onto a familiar, intimate, and immediate world whose relationships carry the same emotional and psychological turmoil as modern ones, while simultaneously occupying a strange world which, the longer the reader inspects and inhabits it, becomes quite other. The reader is lured into identifying with the protagonist and his lover; however, once he understands the importance of social class for Catullus and Lesbia, their very different ages (he was in his twenties, she in her mid-to-late thirties) and the significance of these two factors in historical context, the poem begins to look quite different.

First: because of the relatively low life expectancy in Late Republican Rome, the age gap would be a generational one. Second: in Roman culture of the Late Republic, a marriage might be impossible because of differences in class; in this case, Clodia Metelli was of a higher class than Catullus, an affluent young man from the provinces. An affair, however, would be tolerated. Today, these are private matters, for the judgment of individuals. For the modern-day reader approaching the poem anew, unfamiliar with its cultural nuances, there is a risk: encouraged by the poem's seeming familiarity and the apparent simplicity of the lovers' situation, he is lured into an act of cultural appropriation, eliding the poem's historical reality. The seduction of biographical reading has led to the popular notion that Catullus is 'accessible', or more accessible than other Latin poets of that period, that he is more 'like us', preternaturally modern. In reality the situation is more complex and problematic than it first seems.

The order in which we should read these poems is just as uncertain as the biography of the poet. Indeed, the information available follows a similar pattern: there is just enough evidence to support an authorial ordering and not quite enough to mark that evidence with a stamp of certainty. Who arranged the poems? The poet, or some later, unknown editor or editors? This translation holds to the 'three-book' structure favoured by many scholars of recent years, from T. P. Wiseman to Marilyn Skinner, a structure rejected by other scholars and translators including A.L. Wheeler and D.F.S. Thomson.

The 'three-book' structure tends towards authorial ordering, with some possible later editorial intervention. The translations in this volume follow the guidance of the commentaries, particularly that of Thomson in 1998, the most recent commentary on the source text. My versioning of Catullus breaks the three books into three accepted groupings: polymetrics (Poems 1–60), the long poems on marriage (61–64), and the elegies and epigrams (65–116). Most translations present all 116 as one continuous text, but there have been various attempts to re-order them. The more extreme orderings either attempt a kind of thematised poetic biography (Jacob Rabinowitz) or corral the poems strictly by theme (Josephine Balmer). One thing revealed by these re-orderings is how lines, phrases and whole passages are occasionally repeated. When they appear side-by-side the poems start to become repetitious and boring, and somehow lose their energy. Indeed, what becomes clear is that the poems need to be dispersed through a sequence, so that Catullus's reflections on love, politics, friendship and so on develop across and through the body of work, across all three 'books', revealing (to some extent) authorial intent in the arrangement of the poems as they are.

Other evidence for authorial ordering is tantalising. Perhaps most compelling is the account of critic and translator Charles Martin, who characterises the patterning of the poems and how they 'speak' to one another across the span of the texts as chiastic: for example, Poem 61 (on marriage) 'speaks' to Poem 68 (on adultery). The poems also use chiasmus internally, for example Poem 57, which is topped and tailed by the same line. Martin demonstrates the chiastic patterning in Poem 64, where the eight scenes of the poem create a form of chiastic framing:

i. The courtship of Peleus and Thetis (lines 1–31)
ii. The wedding feast, Part i (lines 32–50)
iii. Ariadne's search (lines 51–116)
iv. Ariadne's lament (lines 117–202)

Bridge: The Judgment of Jove (lines 203–207)

v. Aegeus' lament (lines 208–250)
vi. Iacchus' search (lines 251–265)
vii. The wedding feast, Part ii (lines 266–382)
viii. Conclusion (lines 383–410)

The crucial moment comes at the 'bridge', when Jove delivers his judgment on Theseus's neglect of Ariadne and his failure to replace his ship's black sail with a white one, as his father asked (a signal of Theseus's triumphant return after slaughtering the Minotaur). The poem hinges on line 205, the central line to the poem and a pivot within the three 'books': 'the Heavenly Power nodded unstoppable / approval' – a line that seems straightforwardly positive, a god granting a wish to Ariadne, but which leads to the immediate suicide of Aegeus, and a darkening of the second half of the poem and of 'book three'. These kinds of decisions on the ordering of the poems seem more like those of an author than a later editor. They are also choices consistent with the poems' *internal* logic and aesthetic, and therefore more likely authorial than editorial. In short, alternative arrangements of the poems are simply not as convincing, or as successful, as the ordering of the three books, as they have been handed down.

In the present volume, the differences in metrics between these 'books' are shadowed by differences in syllable count, to produce a line-by-line translation. My version of the first book, in which Catullus uses a variety of metres, is the freest in its treatment of the poems' literal meanings, physical shapes and layout. These liberties allowed me to embrace the wider importance of Catullus in modern culture; for instance, my versions of Poems 16, 25, and 48 echo lines of Frank O'Hara, whose poems change the reader's view of New York City 'like having Catullus change your view of the Forum in Rome' (Allen Ginsberg). So these translations try for cultural equivalence as well as textual accuracy. They show that Catullus's poems are in dialogue with current and recent poetries, and suggest Catullus's important influence on the development of anglophone poetries down the centuries since the Renaissance, when Catullus was first Englished.

In the second and third books this shadowing is much stricter. Here my versions hug closer to the originals line-by-line, reflecting a new astringency in the rhythm and metre as a darker, bitterer tone develops. 'In poetry', wrote Robert Lowell in his introduction to *Imitations*, speaking of what, in essence, translation must achieve, 'tone is of course everything'. If this translation aspires to achieve one thing, it is to register the shifts of tone in the original. It became clear, in the process of working away at the translations in this volume, that a unique quality of Catullus's 'books' is this shifting tone, in tonal weight, away from the lightness of the polymetrics, through the more mature 'wedding' poems (is there a sense here of the poet taking life more seriously?), to the darker tone of 'book three', darkened by the death of the poet's brother, whose absence looms over the final book; by the poet's resignation to the withering of his relationship with Lesbia; and later by the barbed, sometimes desperate, often violent epigrams.

Hand-in-hand with the work's metrical groupings and tonal modulations are its shifts in diction (which similarly tack and veer within a poem or a single line), its soundings of voice (in the form of nuanced raising and lowering), and its complications of syntax. These shifts, soundings and complications give the 'books' characteristic dimensions and unique signatures that a simple division of the poems by their metrics would not. This is why shadowing the later texts closely, line-by-line, was crucial. It allowed me to preserve the meaning of the poem at a microtextual level, to retain the complexity and sophistication of the originals. A good example is Poem 97, which has been somewhat overlooked by critics because of its extreme obscenity, but which shows why line-by-line translation is important when it comes to understanding Catullus's poetry and the unique movement of his line. Poem 97 is a rhetorical *tour de force*, using the elegiac couplet as its vehicle, which gains momentum as it unfolds line-by-line, one image opening onto the next, from the outrageous to the grotesque, before coming to rest in almost surrealist fantasy. The obscenity of the poem acts as a screen, as a form of bathos or exercise of the non-poetic, to mask the poem's aesthetic sophistication.

My focus on the *differences* between the three 'books', between the various genres within them, and on the poems' intricate shifts in tone, voice and mood, have not been as much a focus of earlier translations. Previous translations have tended to homogenise the poems, flattening their voice and tone. But translators that elide these subtleties, these difficulties, reduce the essential texture of the work. This translation attempts to shadow the original with the purpose of highlighting and revealing these features of the source text as fully as possible. Approaches as different as Josephine Balmer's thematic ordering, Peter Whigham's William Carlos Williams versioning, the Zukofskys' homophonic soundings, all tend towards their own totalising homogeneity.

The purpose of this volume is to add to the conversation between different translations of Catullus. What is clear is that Catullus's 'books' have come to occupy a unique place in the canon of Englished poetry. The text of the 116 poems is translated in its entirety from the late nineteenth century onwards (and increasingly by poets). Two fundamental ambiguities – Catullus's biography, and the ordering of the poems – turn each new attempt to translate Catullus over the centuries into a reflection of the cultural, literary, moral and emotional needs of the translator and, to an extent, his or her times. A translation of Catullus is as much a new perspective on Catullus as on ourselves, our life and culture. There is a vacuum left by a lack of facts about the poems and the poet, and a generation of conjecture rushes energetically to fill it. Each conjecture is inevitably a product of the translator's own foibles, predispositions and epoch.

Via Petrarch, and the sixteenth- and seventeenth-century

English translations of the 'kiss' and 'sparrow' poems, Catullus has had a huge influence on the shaping of English love poetry. And therein lies the challenge. Because Catullus's poetry forms a significant strand of our shared poetic DNA, a poet working in English must first translate Catullus in order to understand his or her own work and the work of their generation.

## WORKS CITED

Josephine Balmer (translator), *Catullus: Poems of Love and Hate* (Tarset: Bloodaxe Books, 2004)

Daisy Dunn, *Catullus' Bedspread: the Life of Rome's Most Erotic Poet* (London: William Collins, 2016)

Brad Gooch, *City Poet* (New York: Alfred A. Knopf, 1993)

Robert Lowell, *Imitations* (London: Faber and Faber, 1962)

Charles Martin, *Catullus* (New Haven: Yale University Press, 1992)

Jacob Rabinowitz (translator), *Catullus's Complete Poetic Works* (Dallas, Texas: Spring Books, 1991)

M.B. Skinner, *Catullus' Passer: The Arrangement of the Book of Polymetrics* (Salem, New Hampshire: Ayer Company, 1992)

D.F.S Thomson, *Catullus* (Toronto: University of Toronto Press, (rev.) 1998)

A.L. Wheeler, *Catullus and the Traditions of Ancient Poetry* (London: Cambridge University Press, 1964)

Thornton Wilder, *The Ides of March* (Harmondsworth: Penguin, 1961)

T.P. Wiseman, *Catullus and his World: A Reappraisal* (Cambridge: Cambridge University Press, 1985)

Celia and Louis Zukofsky (translators), *Catullus* (London: Cape Goliard Press, 1969)

*Book One*

# 1

To whom do I send my pretty little sequence
buffed up this very minute with light-grey pumice?

To you, of course, Cornelius, for only you
were friend enough to think something of my ditties –

first and only amongst Italians, who'd risk
chronicle The Whole Story in three episodes,

well-read, by God, an obvious labour of love;
keep my booklet (trim and slender) for all it's worth –

let us pray, Great-Good-Lady patroness on high,
it'll live longer than one trip around the block.

# 2

Sparrow, her pet, my darling's darling,
whom she always plays with on her lap,

to whose peck peck she offers her fingernail
pushing or prodding to grip harder,

when on a whim all glistening eyes
she fancies my charisma and play,

I expect that as her love-ache ebbs,
she finds a little consolation for the hurt

to play with you as she does – I wish –
and brighten each sad care my heart beats with!

# 3

Go on, cry, you Cupids and Venuses,
and you beautiful people of the World.

My dearest girl's sparrow has passed away,
my darling's darling, her petted sparrow,

that she loved more than her own eyes:

he was sweet as honey, could read her mind
as easily as a daughter her mother's;

her lap was all the world he dreamt of;
hopping here and now there, this and that way

piping his song to her and her alone.

Now his flight is a one-way trip only
into darkness where no-one's known return.

Damn you to Hell, dreadful agents of Orcus,
for destroying all beautiful things,

what a darling sparrow you've stolen
(what awful cruelty! Sad little thing!);

you've done what you did, my dear girl welled-up;
her poor little eyes burning with the tears.

# 4

The craft before you, fellow citizens,
declares he was the quickest of vessels,

for speed unsurpassed, no lumber more limber,
would yield not one chance to passing clippers

with lightening flight of paddle and sail.
The Adriatic's rejections he rejects

tossed to its beaches, the Cycladic islands,
illustrious Rhodes, Propontis trembling drenched

in Thracian hurricanes, or the blackening gulf
of Pontus, where he, shortly to be a skiff,

was once dense follicles, topped Cytorus
rattling with chatter other leaves close by.

Pontic Amastris and box-full Cytorus,
this craft says you know what was and what is.

You know. He's positive you recall his birth
long ago, your pinnacle of pinnacles,

it was in your seas he first wet new blades,
and from that place cutting through wild ocean

bore his captain as the winds offered themselves
first to port then starboard, or Jupiter

fell full astern filling both sails together.
No promises were made to the land-gods

on his behalf when after all else he sailed
straight from oceans up this freshwater lake.

But that's all dead and gone; today he grows old
gracefully, totally devoted to you,

the twin Castor, and to the twin of Castor.

# 5

Let's *really* live, Lesbia, which is to love,
and tot up the rumours and grumblings of grey,
old men, to be worth nothing but one sou.
Suns will set and suns will rise for evermore,
for us, finally, our short life snuffed out,
one night, infinite, to sleep the big sleep.
Give me a thousand kisses, then one hundred,
then a thousand, then a second hundred more,
a thousand without a break, and a hundred –
then, when we've totalled up thousands on thousands,
we'll throw them in the air to lose the knowledge,
so no bad person control us with knowing
the grand equation of the sum of our kisses.

# 6

Flavius, if your sweetheart were not lacking
charm and coarse, you'd want to tell Catullus all
about it, and wouldn't be able to stop.
The thing is you've fallen for some common bitch
sickly to look at, but you just won't own up.
For you are not celibate in the night, acting
dumb won't help when your boudoir screams at the top
of its voice, heady with bouquets, Syrian
fragrance, pillows left and right flattened out, and
the shambling bed half-busted shuffles around
on its vibrato, shaky jigging about.
There's no future to your taciturnity.
You may well ask why. You wouldn't seem so clapped out
if you weren't involved in some monkey business.
So spill the beans, for the better or for worse
I want to celebrate you and your lover
to heaven with the force of my funny verse.

# 7

Your question, the total count of your kisses,
Lesbia, to satiate me, and the rest:
as many as there are Libyan sands out
there in lasarpicium-rich Cyrene,
reaching from the sweltering oracle of
Jupiter to the divine grave of Battus;
or as counted a multitude across night's
soundless stars overseeing secret lovemaking.
That's the sum of kisses kissed on kisses kissed.
These would more than satiate insane Catullus:
too numerous for busybodies to add up,
or the wicked to spread vile rumours of.

# 8

Poor Catullus, quit kidding yourself just quit
now know you've lost by admitting the losing.

There was a time when the sun shone all day long on you;
when you followed where the girl led you loved by us all as well

as we who never loved no one before. No not never nor after.
Never.

There were plenty of the 'good times' to go around
and you wanted them all and she wanted them

from sun up to sun down it was as good as it gets.
From here on in she's not up for it and nor should you be,

you jerk, don't scuttle after what runs away faster,
don't do it. It's make your mind up time and stand firm.

Ciao, my pretty. And so today Catullus stands firm
Won't say a word or come looking if you're not willing.

But you'll be sorry when nobody calls, mark my words.
God damn you love what kind of life are you looking for?

Who's calling you pretty now? What kind of guy touches you up?
Who will call you 'my love' my love? Whose will you be called?

Who will you kiss? And whose lips do you get to bite at next?
But you, Catullus, you with your mind made up stand firm.

# 9

Dearest Veranius, best friend of them all,
standing out three hundredfold from the rest –
actually home at last to your household gods,
your close-knit brothers and elderly mother.
You really are? This makes me happy, happy!
Seeing you safely return and hear tales
of Iberia, places, peoples, daily
lives, in your own words, I'll draw you close to me,
kissing your delicious mouth and lovely eyes.
Oh, add up all the happy shiny people,
Who's more happy, more shiny, right now, than me.

# 10

Dearest Varus caught me mooching about the Forum,
insisted I attend visiting hours with his girl.
A right bimbo I thought, on first impression,
but not without intelligence or lacking charm.
On our arrival we chatted through various
sorts of stuff, covering a range of issues:
what the news was of Bithynia, how was
life over there, did I make much money.
Truthfully I retorted, not for praetors
nor for *aides-de-camp* was there any way
they could strike a deal, nor were they the richer,
even more so if your praetor's a bugger,
one who didn't care a sod for his long-suffering aides.
'All the same,' they say, 'you definitely purchased
what everyone knows as the indigenous
resource – bearers.' Determined to look good
to the girlfriend and shine out over the rest,
'Of course,' I say, 'it wasn't all bad where I was,
against the odds of selecting a poor province
I did manage to pick up eight strapping lads.'
If the truth were known there wasn't one, here or
there, capable of shouldering and heaving
the bust leg of a broken down bed-chair.
At this point the teenage dirtbag chimes in with
'My dearest Catullus, let me borrow them
for a bit, I need bearing to the temple
of Serapis.' 'Hold on a minute,' I say
to her, 'what I said a moment ago, those
lads – I must be losing my mind – a slip –
my friend Cinna – Gaius – they're his purchase.
Anyway, why should I give a damn, mine or his?
I get the use of them whenever I please.
But you are a right pain, a disaster area,
who won't let the slightest of things pass you by.'

# 11

Furius and Aurelius, Catullus's *compadres*,
whether he journeys to the outer reaches of India,
where the long coastline lies wide open to faraway echoes
    of Eoan waves,

or to the Hyrcani with those voluptuous Arabs,
or to the Sacae, or to the quivering Parthians,
or to the lowlands dyed all the colours in the Nile
    Delta's seven mouths,

or whether he plots his route traversing the vast Alps,
taking in the sights which tell tales of Caesar's greatness,
the Frankish Rhine, plus those barbarously daubed Brits –
    the end of the World –

these adventures the pair of you are tough enough
to share with me (and heaven knows what else happens),
seek out my dearest and hand her this short note with
    some none too kind words:

go on, let her live with her lovers forever,
all at once grabbing three hundred in her arms,
true to none, over and over busting the nuts
    and guts of the lot;

she should not expect my love as yesterday's,
which because of her, topples like a slender
bloom at the far end of tilled land, being caught
    on a plough's sharpness.

## 12

Asinius Marrucinus, your left hand
inelegant as we imbibe and chatter,
whipping table napkins from engrossed diners.
You reckon you're clever – inept is the truth,
frankly, it's sordid and it's so distasteful.
You don't believe me? Then believe Pollio,
your brother, happy to have your wrongdoing
paid off with real talent; he's overflowing,
a young man of *le mot juste*, a charmer too.
Stand by: three hundred hendecasyllables,
or you mail, by return, my table napkins.
I'm not worried by what they cost so much as
they were a present from my dear *compadres*,
Saetaban table napkins, dispatched from Spain
by Fabullus and Veranius, a gift:
how can I not, therefore, love them deeply, as
I love my Veranius and Fabullus.

# 13

A fine supper for my Fabullus with me
here, in a day or two, should the gods say so,
so long as you offer a fine, sumptuous
meal and don't leave out the dazzling young filly,
and the vino, all sorts of salt and laughter.
If, as I've said, my dear boy, you offer all
this, you'll eat finely, for your Catullus's
purse is woven entirely from spiders' webs.
But, in exchange, you'll receive my love, full-on,
or what is more subtle, and more delicious,
for I'll provide the scents gifted to my love
by all the Venuses and all the Cupids;
on the instant you catch the fragrance you'll beg
the gods, Fabullus, to be re-born just nose.

## 14

If I didn't adore you more than mine own
eyes, wittiest Calvus, I'd hate you for this
gift with a hate beyond that Vatinius;
is it something I did or something I said?
You've done me to death, infested with poets –
gods in heaven pile evil on that client
who mailed you such a gallery of suspects.
If, I surmise, this new and ingenious
work donated by that academic Sulla,
then no, I bear no malice, I'm pleased as punch
that all your good deeds are not gone for nothing.
Good god, what a grim and terrible booklet!
And this the article you mailed Catullus
to knock him off on the day that comes after –
the Saturnalia, the great day of joy!
No, no, no you prankster, this won't be the end:
at daybreak I'll be off down the booksellers
to draw up that venomous crap out of the likes
of Caesius, Aquinus and Suffenus –
and with these as your price, pay you, tit for tat.
As for you, you shower, back in your box you
go, to where your flat feet hobbled this way from,
vermin of our epoch, bad versifiers!

# 14b

If there are any of you out there willing
to view my little bits of trash, who won't shrink
away upon running your hands over it . . .

# 15

I place my all in trust to you, and my love,
Aurelius, and request a small, good deed:
that if with your total Being determined
you maintain a thing fresh and undefiled,
then you'll hold my sweet boy, safely protected.
I'm not thinking of the common people, I've
no worries about those bustling here and there
around the market place and doing deals,
you're the one I fear, you and your massive prick,
ever present hazard to good and bad boys.
Wave the damn thing in whatever direction
you like when you're walking out on the pull,
this particular boy leave out just this once.
But if malice or your loss of the senses
motivates you, you bastard, to betrayal,
an offensive act against my very life,
how I fear for you, the sticky end you'll come to!
With feet bound apart and the arsehole spread wide
rammed to brim full of radishes and mullet.

# 16

(Aurelius in the gob) I'll take on all comers as only
I know how to fuck (Furius up the ass) the both

of you read my poems backward but can't read me

so just watch it – you think I'm a bird, don't you?
If the *real* poet should be chaste his poems needn't be –

then they should rub salt with charm – then,
and only then, when like a poofy truck driver

not decent, my verses might incite an itch you can't
scratch, some action in the grey-haired old fuckers

in need of hip replacements, but you who read my lips
for a thousand kisses are mistaken about my manhood:

up the ass or in the gob, I'll take on all comers.

# 17

Colonia! Desirous of a long bridge for fun and games,
prepared to jump up and down, but scared of the trembling uprights
of this long, ancient footbridge buttressed with recycled piles,
at the risk it collapses backwards, consumed by surrounding filth –
pray a fine bridge be constructed to meet your heart's every need,
resilient to support even Salisubsalian
rites, allow me one real laugh-out-loud moment, Colonia!
There's this close neighbour of mine who I'd like to see tipped head
        first,
slap bang wallop, arse over tit, off your bridge into the muck,
just at the place where the entire bog hole is deeper, blacker,
sulphurous in its stench, a lurid mass of weed and algae.
This one's a right bloody fuckwit without a clue, no more than
a toddler, two years old, cradled in his daddy's arms dreaming.
Though he's married to a young lady approaching perfection,
and a girl fuller of life than the naughtiest little kid,
who requires a more diligent eye than the darkest of grapes,
he doesn't care she plays about as she likes, like he can't see.
And he doesn't stand up for himself, laid low as an alder,
down a drain crippled, as by a sharp Ligurian woodsman,
sentient of all the World as if it never had existed.
My nomination for fool sees no evil, hears no evil,
he's clueless, lost to who he is, even if he *is* at all.
This one's the one I'm dying to hurl head first off of your bridge
to find out if all of a sudden he can be shocked out of
laziness, drop his supine being there in the filthy silt
just as a mule has her shoe dragged off and stuck in the mud.

# 21

Aurelius, the father of appetites,
not only today's, but of those bygone days,
those that are and down all tomorrow's decades:
you're determined to arse-fuck my lovely boy:
not quietly either: you stick to him, giggling
away, up close, covering all the angles.
No joy I'm afraid: despite planning behind
my back, I'll beat you to it with your gob full.
You'd best pipe down if you've been gorging away.
What irks me is that boy will come to know all
you know about eating it and drinking it.
So desist while you still have some decency,
otherwise you'll end up with a great gobful.

## 22

Suffenus, with whom you are not unacquainted, Varus,
is a charming man full of fine talk, urbanity,
and, simultaneously, productive with verses,
ten thousand lines at the last count. Then add the difference:
not the usual scrawl on scraps, like the rest of us –
*au contraire*: regal pages, virginal papyrus,
spotless new rolls, crimson ties to handsome end-covers,
the whole lot smoothed with pumice, lined up true to the lead.
One reads the stuff, this charming man of urbanity,
Suffenus, comes out an ordinary goat-milker,
cloth-eared, and he's *so* other, *so* out of himself.
We deduce what from this? A sophisticated wit
one minute, if anything sharper (is *that* possible?)
in the same breath sounds more hayseed than a hillbilly
nevertheless, the moment he turns versifier,
he's so self-satisfied when versifying verses,
he's so full of himself, and he's so self-regarding.
Evidently, everyone harbours that illusion,
each in some petty manner of speaking, *Suffenus*,
each to his own idiosyncratic foible –
unknowing of the weight you carry on your shoulders.

# 23

Furius, you possess no slave or wallet,
not an arachnid, insect, or firewood,
but a father *and* a stepmother are yours
with gnashers hard enough to devour flint-stone.
What a wonderful life you spend with father
and the old fella's dried stick of a woman.
No surprise there – a happy family in
rude health, settled tummies without a care in
the World, no fires, no dilapidated homes,
no domestic violence or poisoning,
or other dangerous possibilities.
In any case, your bodies dry as old bones,
or drier even than that, if such a thing
exists, with freezing cold, sunshine, dieting.
So how come you're not so fit and well-off?
You've never broken into a sweat or drooled,
no gobbing, no sneezing, you've kept your nose clean.
Now that's clean, clean, clean, and what's cleaner than clean,
an arsehole more polished than a saltcellar;
you can't be taking a dump more than ten times
a year, desiccated as beans, dry as stone,
if you squeezed it between the palms of your hands
you wouldn't force dirt under your fingernails.
These are fine endowments indeed, Furius,
neglect them not, nor disown these great riches,
and desist pursuing me for the hundred
thousand, as you're doing absolutely fine.

## 24

Oh you, fullest bloom of all Juventii,
those alive and kicking, those been and long gone,
and all those yet to come over the decades,
I'd prefer you pass on Midas's fortune
to this one possessing neither slave nor wallet
than you permit the man to make love to you.
'How? Is he not a charmer?' you inquire. Yes:
he's a charmer alright, no slave, no wallet.
Belittle and rationalise this away:
he remains without a slave or a wallet.

# 25

Thallus, you shirt-lifter
        softer than a honey bunny's fur

or a goosey-gander's feather
        or an ear lobe floppy

as an old codger's todger
        blowy cobwebs hang about

Thallus, you money grabber
        by moonlight flap wildly as a Force Ten

when the goddess of thieves preys and pries
        *objets d'art* from sleepy hosts

give me back that cloak you swooped
        on when my back was turned

and my Spanish napkins (the finest) and the Bithynian tablets
        you boast *your* family silver

you filthy philistine! Give them back
        or else – you light-fingered Johnny –

you'll find your pretty little ass
        and soft dannies ruddy-branded by the lash

of my whip, tossing a little
        skiff on a tidal wave out in Hurricane Sebastian, you will.

## 26

Oh Furius, your little country mansion
not credited with breezes from west or south
nor with brutish easterlies and northerlies,
overblown at fifteen thousand sesterces.
A draught guaranteed to make your toes curl up!

## 27

Boy-minister of good old Falernian
splash me out a goblet of drier vintage,
*grande dame* of ceremonies Postumia
orders, who's merrier than merry wine.
You waters be wherever you want to be,
wine's ruin off you go, live with teetotallers,
this man here is untainted Thyonian.

## 28

Piso's *compadres*, the penniless cohorts,
carrying lightened loads and travelling light,
dearest Veranius and my Fabullus,
how's tricks? Have you put up with starvation,
vinegary wine and freezing for that deadbeat?
Does your bookkeeping enter the little gains,
like mine, stacked to the left as loss? Slaving for
my praetor I'd tot my spending as earnings.
Oh Memmius, you really fucked me over,
buggered me completely and without concern.
So, the pair of you are stuck, as I see it,
long suffering a similar giant prick,
shafted. Look out for high-born associates,
pray the gods and goddesses mete out foul
obscenity on Romulus and Remus!

# 29

Who can look on this, who can put up with *this*,
except the unashamed or greedy punters?
Marmurra possessing all transalpine Gaul
and what far-distant Britain used to possess?
You homo, Romulus, look on, and let this go?
When there he is overblown, overpowering,
struts his stuff through all and sundry's wedding bed,
arrogant as a white dove or Adonis,
You homo, Romulus, look on, and let this go?
Then *you* are unashamed, greedy, a punter.
Was this ledger *it*, oh leader of leaders,
what drove you off the edge, the final points west?
Was *this* the case? Your dissipated nob of knobs
might gulp down twenty to thirty million?
What is cock-eyed liberalism but this?
Hasn't he fucked up and guzzled more than his lot?
In the first place he blew his family's loot,
for seconds Pontic spoils, then polished off for
dessert Spanish booty, says the golden Tagus.
Are the riches of Gaul and Britain at risk?
Why the hell coddle that one, the pair of you,
good for nothing but devouring whole lands?
Was *this* the ledger, truly great citizens,
as in-laws, you trashed the whole republic for?

## 30

Alfenus forgetful, leading astray your faithful *compadres*,
do you show no mercy, no empathy for your close *confidant*?
So it has come to this false betrayal without hesitation?
You conceive treachery, sinning placates those that dwell above us?
So you neglect me and abandon me in all my wretchedness?
What is there to be done? Ah, pray show me who can men rely on?
Certainly, my false friend, you insisted I hand my Being over,
reeling me in to love, making it up as if there were no risk.
Now you are backtracking from all you said and all the things you did,
tossed away on the wind in uselessness, reduced to mere vapour.
If you have forgotten the gods recall, and Good Faith recalls all,
and before too long you'll be sorry for every little deed done.

# 31

Of all islands, Sirmio, and peninsulas

you are the pearl of all the two Neptunes'
crystal-clear lakes and salt-rich oceans

how ecstatic I am – what delight to gaze on you again

it's hardly credible, the flat lands of Thynia and Bithynia
pushed well behind me, to rediscover you safe and sound.

Oh, what a joy to have packed troubles off when the mind,
dog-tired, dumps duty (that baggage) in the road where it belongs

– foot-sore, home at last, we truly have arrived at our own front door,
and thank the gods to rest our weary heads between the sheets, home

again home again jiggerty-jig, with it all worth the candle.
Hello, gorgeous! Sirmio, aren't you happy your Master's

happy too – lapping, glittering Lydian waters –

laughter in the ripples laughs all the way home.

## 32

Pretty please, my dear little sweetie, you will,
my sweetheart, my high-class beauty, pretty girl,

ask me around *tout de suite*, postprandial.
And if you do ask me round make it easy:

be certain nobody slides your bolt across,
don't you go slipping out for the hell of it

either but remain indoors, ready ourselves
for nine flying fucks one on top of the other.

So, if you're up for it call me over

I'm ready for you, supine, horizontal,
stuffed to the gills, cock huge, bursting pants and flies.

# 33

Most distinguished wide-boy of the public baths,
daddy Vibennius and your bummer son –
for the daddy's right hand might be grubbier
but the boy's arsehole is all the more hungry –
why don't you bugger off to exile in some
shithole, of daddy's light fingers we all and
sundry know, whilst you sonny boy, cannot trade
your hirsute shit box for one or two bits!

# 34

The purest boys and girls are we,
with Diana our guardian.
* * * * * * * * * * * * *
and young girls form a chorus.

Daughter of Latona, greatest
offspring of greater Jupiter,
who your mother gave birth to close
by the Delian olive,

you became mistress-of-the-peaks
and the verdant, sprouting woodlands,
and the long-deserted scrublands,
and the babbling rivulets.

You are named Lucina Juno
by those in labour of childbirth,
you are known as night's Trivia,
Luna of the stolen light.

You, goddess, mark out month by month
the year's annual direction,
filling to the brim the farmer's
store with fresh fruit and produce.

By whichever name pleases you
you will be praised, as in bygone
days to shield from all the evils
descendants of Romulus.

# 35

Dear papyrus, gently nudge the poet
of love, my *compadre*, my Caecilius –
set out for Verona, leave behind Novum
Comum's city wall, and the Larian shores.
I need him to cast his mind over certain
reflections of a friend known to both of us.
So, if he shows his good sense he'll consume
the miles, even if a lovely girl calls
a thousand times over, her arms locked around
his neck, begging him defer his departure.
There's one, right now, if the truth be rightly told,
loves him madly and without reserve.
From the day she looked into that fragmented
segment of the *Mistress of Dindymus* fires
of love have consumed the sad girl to her core.
I feel for you, girl, more refined than Sappho
the Muse, as Caecilius manufactures
a great fragment to begin his 'Magna Mater'.

## 36

Those cacky sheets of Volusius's *Annals*

uphold the promise you're made for: my dearest
made a promise to the holies Venus and Cupid

that if I were to return to her and quit
chucking the vicious iambics about

she might just despatch the worst possible verses

from the World's Worst Poet to the hop-along Devil
for kindling olive branches at the poet's own funeral.

The Worst Girl in the World concocted this vow
as a joke for the gods – and it's too cocky by half.

So, goddess of the deep and of the wide and of the blue,
who resides at the holiest Idalium, the wide

open waterways at Urii, at Acona, reedy Cnidus,
at Amathus and Golgi's shrine

at Dyrrachium and all the pubs and clubs of Hadria,

cross this vow off as a contract totted up and paid,
unless you deem the jape without merit or credit.

Meanwhile into the fire you go, fuel the flames
you bunch of hayseed platitudes:

Volusius's *Annals* pure bullshit every one. Page on page.

# 37

That hang out for beasts of the field and all you piss-heads,
nine pillars beyond 'The Brothers" pad (C & P sporting 'party hats') –

do you really think for one minute you're the only ones with a dick?
The only swordsmen to carry a licence to fuck the sweeties wholesale

over and over, all the rest of us stink something rotten – as goats?

Or, perhaps, you lounge-lizards sitting back in your queue
(is it one or is it two hundred of you? whatever!) don't suppose

I wouldn't dare make you eat it at one sitting: I would.

Ponder and reflect, you wankers: I'll daub 'pricks'
and 'cunts' right across the front wall of your inn,

for my sweet girl who slipped from my arms,
who was never loved by anyone as she was loved by me,

for whom I've fought my many great battles has set
up her stall right here right now. She's your lover,

the great and good-hearted, and what's more (the shame
of it) of every back-alley cocksucker and kerb-crawler,

with you, first and foremost, one of those long-haired louts,
son of a buck-toothed Spaniard,

Egnatius, for whom a goatie makes a pretty face (marks
him out), whose teeth are brushed in Spanish piss.

# 38

This is bad, Cornificius, for your dear Catullus
this *is* bad, bloody Herculean it is, and hard graft

indeed every hour of every day it's huge and getting bigger.

As for you, what is the least you can do –
have you shown him the smallest comfort?

God, I'm pissed off with you. What about my love?

Mail a word or two for comfort, I beg of you,
attached to a few tears of Simonides.

# 39

Because Egnatius sports shiny white gnashers
his smile's all about town: while the defence works

the court over, wringing out the sobs he's smiling,
a grief-stricken mother loses her only boy –

there he is again, at the pyre, choppers flashing.
Whatever's going on, all the time, here and there

and everywhere his weakness, this smiling; and not,
if I may say so, with elegance or taste.

So, just a thought, sunshine, matey Egnatius:
if you were a man of Rome, or Tiburtine, or

Sabine, or a porcine Umbrian, a chubby
Etruscan, or a black, toothy Lanuvian,

or of breeding, a Transpadane (one of my sort)
or any other who brushes with spring water,

I'd banish that interminable smiling forever:
nothing's more vacant than a vacuous smile.

But you're a Spaniard, and in Spain you're all

of the same custom with your own piss for toothpaste
each morning, and every tooth every raw gum brushed.

So for teeth whiter than white there's one true test:
the brighter the smile the more piss you'll have drunk.

## 40

Such a derangement of the senses, Ravidus
casts you up on to the razors of my iambs.

Good God, you've advocated none too cleverly,
provoking such dumb-assed quarrelling between us.

Are you really *this* desperate for adulation
from the common people? *This* limelight at all costs?

It's all yours: you've opted to love my lover too.
Pay the toll – my price your reputation, Big Time.

# 41

Ameana, that completely fucked slag,
demands I cough up a straight ten thousand,
the slapper who features less than a straight nose,
consort to the broke debtor of Formiae.
Those nearest and dearest in charge of the woman
must call out the doctors, call in her friends:
the girl's lost her marbles, doesn't stop to ask
the bronze full of images her real worth.

## 42

Come along, hendecasyllables, everyone
of you out of everywhere and every last one.
A cheeky scrubber has taken me for a ride
saying, if you don't mind, she'd rather not hand back
our notebooks – that's more than difficult to swallow.
We need to pursue her, insist she give them up.
You may well ask which one is she? It's that one there
with the inelegant gait and histrionic
cackle, and all the looks of a real French bitch.
So, form a circle now, let's shout together,
'Disgusting hooker hand over the notebooks now,
hand over the notebooks, you disgusting hooker.'
She flips us the 'v's. Ah, the scrubber, the hooker,
or whatever other name-calling you can think of.
But we cannot think the game's over with that.
We can do nothing more I suppose than make her
burn red in the face with complete embarrassment.
Yell at the top of your voices, all together:
'Disgusting hooker hand over the notebooks now!
hand over the notebooks, you disgusting hooker!'
This is getting us nowhere, she doesn't bat an eyelid.
We'll have to adjust our pitch and methodology.
Let's give this a go and see where it might get us:
'Lady of Honour and Purity, my notebooks?'

# 43

Good day, young lady, neither snub-nosed enough
nor with beautiful feet, without the coal eyes,
without the long fingers, without the dry mouth,
hardly with the most beautiful of accents.
Consort to that broke debtor of Formiae,
you the Province announces as the stunner?
In comparison to my Lesbia?
Oh, what times we live in without taste or reason!

## 44

Our homestead, whether Sabine, whether Tiburtine –
so some assert you Tiburtine who care not to
harm Catullus, on the other hand there are those
who stake at all costs you're definitely Sabine –
but if you're Sabine, or perhaps, in fact, Tiburtine,
I was immensely grateful of my sojourn in
suburbia to cure me of a chesty cough,
which were just deserts caused by stomach-churning greed
in my mad-dash rush after exclusive dinners.
For, in my haste and speed to become Sestius's
guest I read his oration opposing Antius,
'the candidate', stuffed with bile and contagion.
Whereupon I came down with a stinking cold and
hacking cough, which wracked me until I retreated
to your haven for remedy, quiet and herb tea.
So now, fit again, I tender grateful thanks
you saw right I not suffer for my misdemeanour.
Nor will I take exception to terrible works
by Sestius, but handling the cold pages visit
sniffles and tickly cough, not on me, but Sestius,
whose invites come once I've read his contagious speech.

# 45

Septimius, with dear, dear Acme held close
on his knee, whispered, 'my dearest one, Acme,
if I'm not driven out of my mind with love,
totally devoted to you forever,
just as mad as a madly 'in love' lover,
let me alone in Libya or baking
India stare out the lion-of-green-eyes.'
Then, with that said, Amore once to the left,
once to the right, atichooed, for good measure.

Acme tipping her head softly backwards,
brushing with a full, velvety bee-sting for lips
the swimming eyes of her young boy sent tipsy,
and she said, 'Septimius, light of my life,
swear our servility to this sole leader,
certain as and as scorching as the keen fire
ignites my tender core and courses through me.'
Then, with that said, Amore once to the right,
once to the left, atichooed, for good measure.

Choosing a sunny path of positive signs,
in love and loving in equal measure:
love-sick Septimius adores Acme above
all your Great Britains and all your Syrias;
for Acme love will out in Septimius,
collecting her complete set of fun and games.
Who's observed two people more beautiful?
In whom does Goddess Venus read more hopeful signs?

# 46

Now springtime returns days to the mildest air,
now the gale-force madness of the equinox
is quieter by the zephyr's welcomed hush.
Take off, Catullus, from Phrygian lowlands
and the enclosed, heat-hazed plains of Nicaea.
Let's head for the dazzling cities of Asia.
Now my heart's aflutter with plans to roam,
now my toes tap in eager anticipation.
*Adieu* to the whole genial entourage
who set out on a long journey from homelands,
wander back via diverse solitary routes.

## 47

Porcius and Socration, Piso's pair, both
light-fingered Johnnys, harbingers of scabies
and appetite, you're held above Fabullus
and my Veranius by *that* upstanding
Priapus? Is it you planning exclusive
dinner-times in daytime whilst my *compadres*
are forced to scrape the alleyways for invites?

## 48

Your eyes sweetened as honey, Juventius –
if they permit me my fill, all-I-can-kiss,
I'd carry on kissing three hundred thousand
fold, nor would I be satiated,
not if the gathering of all our smoochings
were packed more tightly than ripened ears of corn.

# 49

The very best of speakers of Romulus's
genus, of those who went before you, Marcus
Tullius, who are, or shall be in years to come,
a great and heartfelt 'thank you' from Catullus;
he the direst of all the poets in the World,
equally the direst of all the poets
as you are highest of rhetoricians.

## 50

Yesterday, Licinius, didn't we while away the hours
like a couple of naughty schoolboys at my lap top

pissing about together, sniggering at a good joke –
we each in turn whacked off some little ditties,

one in this metre then one more in that for good
measure, just for a laugh to match excellent wine.

After *that* you bet I left all fired up
by your wit and charm, Licinius, so much

so poor little me lost his appetite for dinner,
nor could I find relief with a lie down or shut-eye,

but tossed and turned in bed all night
long, longing for daybreak that I might

return to your side and chatter away some,

arms and legs aching after all that
I lay in bed more or less half-dead

and wrote this trifling poem for you my dear
so you can see the state you've left me in,

don't be rough, pretty please, don't chuck out my prayers
I beg of you, my nearest and dearest: there's always Nemesis

who might demand payback with menaces –
she's the bitch goddess you don't want to mess with.

# 51

I reckon that man appears a god's equal,
or, if I may, that man is a superior
to the gods, sat opposite looking who listens
      and hears you over

and over, it's your pretty laughter that wrenches
me, wretched, totally of my senses, Lesbia,
simultaneously, when I gaze up at you
      I lose all talent

to chat away, my tongue numb, limbs heated to white-
hot, ears ringing with sounds all of their own accord,
a double nightfall wraps about the twinkling light
      in both my eyes.

Leisure, Catullus, not a good idea for you,
leisure leaves you energised, over-stimulated.
Leisure: the thing that unseated kings, lost and ruined
      magnificent cities.

## 52

What's the use, Catullus? Drop dead right here, right now?
Nonius, that boil, takes up an official seat,
Vatinius lies his way to the consulship.
What's the use, Catullus? Drop dead right here, right now.

# 53

Someone from the crowd made me smile today:
who, once my dear Calvus had wonderfully
explicated the crimes of Vatinius,
punched the air and cheered in astonishment,
'Good God, that little upstart can talk the talk!'

## 54

Otho's dickhead (exceedingly minuscule),
and then, Rusticus, your thighs, huge and unwashed,
and Libo's passing wind, silent but deadly –
I hope against hope all these things bring discomfort
to you and re-animated Fufidius . . .

## 54b

You'll be furious at my whiter than
white iambics, again, our one Great Leader.

## 55

We implore you, if it's not over-taxing,
reveal to me your darkest whereabouts.
I've been looking here and there in the Campus
Minor, the Circus Maximus, at the sign
of booksellers, the most sacred place of Jove.
I took a stroll down the Great Walk as well
my friend, quizzed every little tart there,
but they blinked back innocently enough.
'Turn him in,' I insisted of each one,
'give me Camerius, you sinful lot.'
'Right here,' called one, unlacing her thin slip,
'look here, he's resting between my rosy tits!'
All of this trouble you've been is the work
of Hercules, you're too snobby, *compadre*.
So, let us fix a venue and time, declare
it, commit to it, believe in daylight.
Do the pretty little blondes tether you down?
If you bite your tongue, remain tight-lipped
you'll have frittered away love's harvest.
Venus thrives on the fullness of rhetoric.
In any case, as you like it, zip it,
just as long as I'm cut my cut of your love.

# 56

O a most amusing jape, Cato, how daft,
one you need to know of and titter about!
Laugh you must Cato, loving your Catullus:
it's so, so very amusing, too too daft.
This minute I found my sweet girl's servant boy
knocking one out, so preserve me Dione,
I straight shafted him – Lucky Pierre style!

## 57

Such splendid partners, a right pair of knobs,
Marmurra and Caesar – girly homos, those two.
No surprise. Besmirched in equal measure,
one city-stained, the second Formian,
branded permanently it won't fade away.
Infected the same, these two peas in a pod,
a couple of poetasters to one stool,
one voracious in adultery as his mate,
each in competition over sexy teens,
such splendid partners, a right pair of knobs.

## 58

Caelius, my Lesbia, Lesbia, *the* Lesbia above all,
above all the one and only Catullus loved more

than himself, all his family and all his friends thrown

together, now hangs around street corners and back alleys
popping peas for the great and good-hearted sons of Remus.

# 58b

Were I moulded as Crete's custodian,
nor Ladas, nor feather-footèd Perseus,
nor if I swept aloft astride Pegasus,
nor Rhesus's teamed stallions dazzlingly white –
supplement to these the wingèd, the downy,
and demand the swiftness of full-blown gales:
tie me in to all of these, Camerius
I'd be tired to my bones, dead-beat tired beyond
tired, with repeated exertions after
this interminable hunt, my *compadre*.

# 59

*– Rufa the Bononian fellates Rufulus –*

She's Menenius's wife, you know, the one you spot
from time to time down the crematoria ripping off

a crust or two as it rolls from the half-charred bodies
whilst the undertaker's unshaven slave bangs her rear.

## 60

Was it a lioness from the Libyan foot-hills

or was it Scylla that spat you howling
her vulva which bore a mind so hard

so cruel you dash the prayer from
this believer's lips, oh stony-hearted love?

*Book Two*

## 61

Helicon's inhabitant,
O Urania's offspring,
Who tears away fresh-faced girls
For their grooms, *O Hymenaee Hymen,*
*O Hymen Hymenaee,*

Garland your locks with heady
Sweetness, blooms of marjoram;
Parade the flaming veil
Come happily come, snow-white
Feet lemon-sandaled.

Awakening this lovely
Day declaim the wedding songs
With as sweet a voice, trample
The earth with dance shaking
The burning pine branch.

Junia, pert as Venus,
Idalium's girl facing
The Phrygian magistrate;
Good girl with favourable
Signs, weds Manlius;

Lovely as Asian myrtle
Radiant with flowery stalks
Hamadryades (wood nymphs)
Feed with the fresh morning dew,
Their very own toys.

Come along, quickly arrive,
Take leave of Aonian
Places on the Thespian
Rock, cooling Aganippe
Irrigates above.

Entice the mistress homeward,
Desiring her new partner,
Wrapped about with affection,
As ivy seeks here then there
Embraces the tree.

And you, the rest of the girls
Unmarried, whose day will come,
Sing along with me and in
Tune: *O Hymenaee Hymen,*
*O Hymen Hymenaee,*

That He will readily hear
Calls He occupy the role
Correctly His, Venus's guide,
And conjugate lovers both
Legitimately.

Which god is more suitably
Sought by anxious love-makers?
What deity should beings
Pray to, *O Hymenaee Hymen,*
*O Hymen Hymenaee?*

Anxious fathers pray to you
For the children, young girls slip
Out of their girdles for you,
For you excited bridegrooms
Heed with ready ears.

You have yourself pressed into
The hands of a mannish boy
A fresh-faced girl torn from her
Mother's breast, *O Hymenaee Hymen,*
*O Hymen Hymenaee.*

With you absent Venus can't
Seek the fun celebrity
Permits; yet she's able if
You are willing too. Which god
Challenges this god?

With you absent: childless homes,
Parents' lines discontinued,
Heirless: yet they're able if
You are willing too. Which god
Challenges this god?

Lacking your rituals no
Nation fields patrols at its
Checkpoints: yet it's able if
You are willing too. Which god
Challenges this god?

The door unlocked and flung wide,
Come bride, come. Watch the torches
Shiver, burning follicles
* * * * * * * * * * * *
* * * * * * * * * * * *


* * * * * * * * * * * *
* * * * * * * * * * * *
High-born chastity prevails
To which she is most attuned,
Cries the hard parting.

Stop up your tears. No way, Au-
runculeia, exists the chance
A woman more beautiful
Will witness the clear dawn light
Rise over the seas.

As in the multicoloured
Plots of the rich landowner
The hyacinth stands up straight.
You hesitate, days pass by,
Fresh bride step forward.

Fresh bride step forward. If it
Pleases you hear our requests.
Do you see? Watch the torches
Shiver burning follicles.
Fresh bride step forward.

It is not true: your groom will
Not cheapen himself lying
With some dirty whore, or chase
Ignoble paths by sleeping
Apart from your breast.

And as flexible tendrils
Wrap around next door's trees
So he will be wrapped around
In your arms; but days pass by
Fresh bride step forward.

Divan for those attending
* * * * * * * * * *
* * * * * * * * * *
* * * * * * * * * *
Bed's glistening toe.

Such ecstasies fall his way,
Such huge ecstasies your husband's
Pleasured by as the night passes,
Midday too! But days pass by;
Fresh bride step forward.

Pages! Hold torches skywards
The flaming veil approaches.
Sing along with me and in
Tune, '*Io Hymen Hymenaee io,*
*Io Hymen Hymenaee.*'

Muzzle not the Fescennine
Fun, but let it carry on
Make the smartest page toss nuts
To slave boys once his master's
Love he knows is gone.

Toss nuts to slave boys, lazy
Page, your time is up, for long
Enough you've toyed with nuts. Cease!
Now go serve Talassius.
Lazy page, toss nuts.

Just the other day you swore
At the farm bailiff's wives, page.
Now the barber's attendant
Clips away. Poorest of boys!
Lazy page toss nuts.

You have difficulty, say
Some, foregoing pretty boys –
Forego you must, fragrant groom!
*Io Hymen Hymenaee io,*
*Io Hymen Hymenaee.*

We recognise a licence
For men-about-town was yours,
But none for spouses exists.
*Io Hymen Hymenaee io,*
*Io Hymen Hymenaee.*

And you, new wife, be careful
Denying your man's pleasure –
He'll make for another place.
*Io Hymen Hymenaee io,*
*Io Hymen Hymenaee.*

Look, how opulent a house
(Big and grand) your master's is,
And all this at your service,
(*Io Hymen Hymenaee io,*
*Io Hymen Hymenaee*).

When snowy with old age you'd
Nod assent without question,
Say yes to all and sundry,
*Io Hymen Hymenaee io,*
*Io Hymen Hymenaee.*

Trip golden-heeled over
The lintel, with fine report
Pass via the slick portal,
*Io Hymen Hymenaee io,*
*Io Hymen Hymenaee.*

Gaze on your spouse relaxing
Indoors over a divan
Entirely inclined to you.
*Io Hymen Hymenaee io,*
*Io Hymen Hymenaee.*

A fire-storm sweeps through each
Ventricle of his heart, fierce
As yours, and more intensely.
*Io Hymen Hymenaee io,*
*Io Hymen Hymenaee.*

Release the girl's tender arm
Purple-robed youth this minute;
Released to her spouse's bed.
*Io Hymen Hymenaee io,*
*Io Hymen Hymenaee.*

All of you good, worldly dames
Conjugated with their old
Chaps, help the bride to her seat.
*Io Hymen Hymenaee io,*
*Io Hymen Hymenaee.*

Groom, now you are permitted,
Approach your new wife's boudoir,
Her cheeks radiant as young
White buds of the daisy or
A flaming poppy.

Praise be to the gods, young man
If you aren't as lovely, fair
As she: Venus sees to you,
But days pass by, step forward,
Hold back no longer.

You didn't hold back for long.
You've come already, Venus-
the-Good to aid you. It's plain
What you want, you want the best
Love with no holds barred.

He who calculates each grain
Of African sand, each glint
On glint of the heavenly
Bodies could enumerate
Your great love-making.

Make love as numerously
As possible, shortly spawn
Children. Ancient titles need
Heirs, and along similar lines
Perpetuated.

I want a Little Baby
Torquatus reaching out from
His mother with tiny hands
To 'papa' – happily smile
Little lips opening.

Would he be as Manlius
The image of his father
Obvious to all he meets,
And his face fairly portray
His mother's honour.

Pray his good name evidence
His line from a true mother,
As Penelope the best
Handed on Telemachus's
High reputation.

Slam the doors, virgin slave-girls.
Enough of our joy. But you,
The happy couple, well done,
Enjoy your lives to the full
As wife and husband.

## 62

Venus rises:
        young Turks raise yourselves:
                Venus flickers
High above Olympus,
        long-anticipated.
The moment has arrived,
        up,
        tables groaning:
Here comes the bride,
        here wedding chants to be performed.

        *Hymen O Hymenaee, Hymen here O Hymenaee!*

You girls,
        observe the young Turks?
                Line up opposite.
The bringer of night kindles the Oetaean glow.
Yes,
        without doubt.
            They're keen,
                quick out of the traps!
They spring forward;
        a good chance their song's the favourite.

        *Hymen O Hymenaee, Hymen here O Hymenaee!*

Brothers,
        no push-over victory lies in store.
Listen,
        the birds rehearse their off-by-heart lyrics.
Rehearsals pay back well;
                catchy melody.
No surprises.
        They concentrate their attention.

Meanwhile we think of one thing whilst listening to another;
We lose,
            fair enough;
                        winning needs blood,
                                    sweat and tears,
For the minute bring your thoughts to bear on the job;
They're about to pipe forth,
                        then it's our turn to respond.

*Hymen O Hymenaee, Hymen here O Hymenaee!*

Hesperus, who blazes more fiercely in heaven?
How could you wrench a girl from her mother's bosom
From her mother's bosom wrench a clingy girl,
And pass a virgin over to a hot young buck.
Could an enemy seize a town more viciously?

*Hymen O Hymenaee, Hymen here O Hymenaee!*

Hesperus, who beams more happily in heaven?
Your brightness casts a light over the marriage vows
That fathers promise in advance and grooms promise,
But won't deliver without your blazing overhead.
What moment do gods offer more pleasurable?

*Hymen O Hymenaee, Hymen here O Hymenaee!*

Sisters, Hesperus, has spirited one away
* * * * * * * * * * * * * * * * * * *
* * * * * * * * * * * * * * * * * * *

For as you appear security guards clock on.
Robbers are shrouded by dead of night, you return,
Hesperus, disguised as Eous, shadowing them.
Virgins like to trouble you with made-up stories.
Who cares if, for all their false chatter, you're the one?

*Hymen O Hymenaee, Hymen here O Hymenaee!*

As a flower nurtured by a sheltered garden,
Invisible to the herd, untouched by ploughshares,
Kissed by gusts of wind, stronger for sun, grows in rain,
Countless boys, numerous girls reached out towards it:
For this selfsame bud, stripped between finger and thumb,
Neither the boys nor the girls reach out towards it.
An unsullied young girl enjoys her tribe's constancy;
Her body polluted, losing her purest bud,
She's the object of desire for neither boys nor girls.

*Hymen O Hymenaee, Hymen here O Hymenaee!*

As an unsupported vine creeps over stripped land
Won't reach the heights, won't yield the generous sweet fruits,
Instead weakens, folds in half with the sheer burden
Nearly, nearly brushes root system with freshet;
She uncultivated by farm-hand or the ox:
Yet one by chance hitched up to a caring elm,
She is cultivated by farm-hands and oxen:
An unsullied young girl will grey if neglected,
Yet in due course forges a seemly coupling,
More loved by her spouse, less a nuisance to parents.

You, new wife, dare not to squabble with your partner,
Don't quarrel with the man your father signed you to.
Your mother, your father, your duty – make them proud.
You don't own your honour, your parents own some shares;
Your father dealt a third, your mother a third too,
You receive a third. Don't argue with mum and dad
They signed you away, rich assets for a new son.

*Hymen O Hymenaee, Hymen here O Hymenaee!*

# 63

Across deepest oceans Attis catapulted in his quick yacht,
headlong inland with flight of foot, to approach the Phrygian woods,
pressing forward and through dark woods, the goddess's crowning
    thicket,
and at that point tortured beyond sense, reason blinded beyond logic,
arrowhead razor-sharpened he sliced away his genitals.
So then *she* sensed her limbs useless, severed, lacking his manliness,
even as new blood spattered down, reddening the earth all around –
with the quickest of reactions, white-knuckled she shook the timbrel –
your timbrel, Cybebe, all yours, Matriarch – mysteries on high,
rattling and tapping out deftly, finger-tipped the sonorous hide,
and forthwith she started to sing, a-tremble, to her disciples:

'Up, up and away together, Gallae, to Cybele's tree-tops,
follow me together, lost of Dindymenian Domina,
who were quickly banished from homes, look towards foreign places,
toe my line of reasoning, accomplices on my pathway
have resisted sea currents and the fury of the oceans,
unmanning your own bodies, beyond total disgust for Love:
make ecstatic your goddess's heart with non-stop frenzied dancing.
Expunge all thought of postponement – all together, in my footsteps
to Phrygia, Cybele's home, to the goddess's Phrygian woods –
where voices of cymbals sing out, where tambourines echo reply,
where the Phrygian flautist booms deeper sounds from a curved horn,
where the Maenads garbed with ivy shake their heads in complete
    frenzy,
where with piercing cries blurted loud and clear they play out sacred
    rites,
where wayward followers to the goddess often fled on foot,
towards that place we must trip quick-stepping our way speedily.'

In that moment, no real woman, Attis sang to the company,
the whole troupe cried a-trembling, voices out loud ululating,
where tambourines rattled once more, again cymbals tinkled away,

on jostling, flitting feet the chorus converged towards verdant Ida.
Delirious, wobbly, panting, senseless, breathing her one last breath,
supported by tambourine, Attis unthinking, pressed through dark
    woods,
(a cow undomesticated, throwing off the weight of harness),
for the Gallae keenly to track their leader from her footsteps.
Cybebe's shrine attained, an effeminate lassitude fell
across them, sleepy after strife, huge labour without sustenance:
over tired eyes sleepiness ebbs and flows, enveloping eyes shut,
soothing frantic thoughts with quiet to melt desperation away.
But when the sun, bright, golden-faced, the piercing gaze of his
    warm eyes
scanned across the lucent sky, the harsh ground, the furious sea,
driving away shadowy night with his horses, a team fresh-shod,
then Sleep retreated quickly, (leaving Attis alert, wide awake),
to the Goddess Pasithea, enveloped in her pulsing heart.
So after quiet time and rest, free of overheated panic,
when Attis reflected on those actions she herself had triggered
and saw in the cold light of day what she had come to, what was lost,
in chaotic and teeming thoughts she retraced her steps to the beach,
gazing over desolate seas, there she wept tears copiously,
in this pitiful state she spoke broken-voiced to her motherland:

'Oh my country which created me, oh my country where I was born
and pathetically abandoned, just as fugitive slaves abscond
their masters, and flee light-footed into Ida's dense woodland,
that I might live up in snowfields, amongst animals' frozen dens,
venturing in my distraction to seek their every habitat –
in what direction, whereabouts do I believe you are, my land?
My eyes of their own accord drawn to direct their vision at you,
in this briefest of interludes whilst my senses are free of stress.
Am I to be kidnapped from home, spirited away to these woods?
My motherland, goods and chattels, all acquaintance, family – gone?
Gone from the Forum, palestra, stadium, and gymnasium?
Miserable, miserable soul whose existence is mere grief,
what variant of human have I not metamorphosed into?
I am a woman, I am a young man, I am a juvenile, a boy,
I was the gymnasium's bloom, sweet-scented beauty:

mine were the doorways crowded out, mine were the doorsteps
always warm,
mine were the bouquets of flowers which decorated the household,
as the sun climbed the heavens and I departed my bedroom.
Am I now reckoned slave to the gods, and in service to Cybele?
Am I considered a Maenad, am I half a self, am I unsexed?
Am I to lurk about the snowbound, evergreen slopes of chill Ida?
Am I sentenced to a lifetime beneath Phrygia's dizzy heights
where the deer finds its home in woods, where the wood-foraging
    boar lives?
Now, now I am agonised, now, now full of remorse.'

As soon as this speech was broadcast abroad, loud from her rosebud
    mouth,
conveying unexpected reports to the gods' acute hearing –
then Cybele untied the halter and reins binding her lions,
and provoking the master of herds, leashed on the left, she said:

'Go on,' she urged, 'go on angry beast, ensure insanity vex her,
see her downed by insanity, retreating to my wooded lands,
she who enjoys excess freedoms, over-eager to slip my hold.
Beat your hindquarters with your tail, bite back the trashing of
    yourself,
make sure every compass point is filled with your thundering roar
fearless one, unfurl your yellowy mane from your muscled neck.'

So Cybele furiously declared untying the halter,
the raging animal steeled, incited his angry being,
jumping up, growled out loudly, tramped down surrounding cover.
And as he approached the wetlands of glistening, foamy shore
and encountered effeminate Attis next to the marble sea,
he lunged. She, panicked and routed, a wild thing, retreated to woods:
always to stay, a life sentence, to be forever the slave-girl.

Goddess, great goddess, Cybebe, goddess, Matriarch of Dindymus,
pray all your discord and anger remain distant from my home –
push the rest to insanity, push the rest to pleasure's excess.

## 64

Fir-trees, descendants from Pelion's pinnacles,
so it is rumoured, stroked through Neptune's breakers
to the watery Phasis and Aeetes' borders,
when the finest boys, the backbone of Argive youth
endeavoured hijacking the Colchian fleece,
daring their quick skiff navigate the salt sea Abyss,
pinewood blades brushing over aquamarine,
for them the goddess who rules the mountain cities
constructed the speediest vessel with her fair hands,
interlaced the softwood with hardwood framework;
the original vessel to skim Amphitrite.
Just as soon as the bow had tilled the blustery sea,
oarsman curling wave-tops to foamy whiteness,
faces rose with the surf out of curiosity,
Nereids admiring the phenomenon.
For that day and that day only mariners gazed
upon sea-nymphets rising above foaming
ocean swell, full-frontal, topless, nipples erect.
Then, Peleus flared with passion for Thetis,
then Thetis did not cast aside wedding a human,
then the Father knew Peleus was made for Thetis.

Oh you, born into the best of epochs much missed,
all heroes we salute you, sons of the gods
and noble ladies I salute you one more time!
Again, again I will celebrate you with song.
You above the rest, lucky with the marriage torch,
Peleus, Thessaly's rock, to whom Jupiter himself,
*himself*, god of the gods, relinquished his own love;
did Thetis, gorgeous Nereid, overwhelm
you, did Tethys grant you permission to wed her child's
child, and Oceanus, who clinches the world in one?
Then, as the right moment approached for the couple,
all Thessaly frequented the house, bursting

the palace with delirious company,
each one offering tributes, shiny happy faces.
Cieros a ghost-town; Phthiotian Tempe
Crannon and Larissa – everywhere emptied;
Pharsalus crammed, crowding Pharsalian households.
The countryside deserted, oxen out of shape,
the curling rake no longer guides the creeping vines,
the bull and plough fail to turn over heavy clays,
no secateurs chop back the shades of olive groves,
farm machinery, abandoned, rusts away.

But at the master's house, whichever direction rich
hallways stretch, gleams a vision of gold and silver,
the thrones of white ivory, tables glittering cups,
the entire palace joyous at the rich spectacle.
The centrepiece a marriage-divan fitting
a divinity, ornamented with Indian
ivory inlay, shell-stained, decked out in crimson.

This needlepointed throw picks out ancient characters,
and dexterously depicts their heroism.
Unstoppable, from Dia's wave-echoing beach
Ariadne's gaze on Theseus's quick vessel,
disappearing to a dot, eaten up inside
she scarcely credits witnessing what she has seen,
little wonder this, as on that precise instant
she was snapped out of sleep, discarded on cold sands.
That thoughtless boy escaping to rhythmic oars, tosses
promises overboard into winds' teeth.
At such a distance, Minos's daughter, seaweed about
her feet, frozen bacchant gazing out, pitiful,
gazing on, knocked off balance by surging emotion;
the precious hairband loosens from her long blond hair,
light as a feather her dress slips off her shoulders,
her brassiere drops from full and milky breasts –
all her clothes fell from her body in a heap,
trivia to saltwater breakers about her feet,

uncaring about headbands, uncaring about
dresses, her heart swollen to bursting, Theseus,
all her mind, all her body dependent on you.
Sad thing, where Erycina cast barbed worry
in her heart, who she obsessed with infinite pain,
forever and a day since the rash Theseus
exited Piraeus, its sweeping harbour-mouth,
reaching Gortynia, the outlaw's kingdom.

So the myth goes how vicious diseases visited,
reparation for Androgean's killing,
Cecropia was compelled to select perfect
young girls and men for the Minotaur's table.
His provincial city threatened by injustice,
*himself,* Theseus, preferred to risk his own
body for Athens than endure awful carnage,
Cecropia's walking-death exported to Crete.
So then, entrusting his quick craft to the warm winds
he fetched up at Minos, 'the magnanimous'.
From the first moment the regal daughter gazed on
him, although restricted to her fragrant bedroom,
still cradled in the gentle arms of her mother,
like myrtle propagated by Eurotas
or colours differentiated in Spring,
her first looking lingered longer on him until
her entire body was engulfed, to be consumed
at her very heart, her depths in conflagration.
Sacred boy, maliciously concocting powerful
feelings, mix joy with pain for Man, stony-hearted,
and you, queen of Golgi and verdant Idalium,
on tempestuous oceans you discarded
the girl there, heart on fire, murmuring for the blond guest!
Such huge dread she endured with an exhausted heart!
Repeatedly she grew sallow as gold's reflection,
for Theseus, desperate to challenge the vicious
man-beast sought death or the spoils of victory!
She promised trifles, promises appealing to gods,

mouthing silences to deities above.
As an oak from the tops of Taurus waves its branches,
or a cone-heavy conifer, bark seeping amber,
a hurricane angrily ripping apart
its body – dismembered, upended, crashes,
reducing all to matchwood in its path far and wide,
so Theseus levelled the weighty man-beast, horns
uselessly waving about emptied spaces.
Then back he retraced the pathway to loud acclaim, a
slenderest thread navigating the journey
in case the labyrinthine meanderings
entangle him within incomprehension.

So why do I stray widely from my first poem?
Recall how a daughter deserted a watchful
father, how she deserted a sister, a mother
who loved to distraction her miserable child,
who adored Theseus before all these others?
Or how he stole her away by sea to Dia's
spumy shore, or how he left her sleeping the deep sleep,
heartlessly embarking, no second thoughts?
Frequently, so the myth goes, with her heart consumed,
she would drag out jagged sobs from her deepest being
now at her most wretched, scaling sheerest clifftops
where she could observe clearly the desolate ocean,
or would dash headlong into the choppy sea-surge, legs
exposed, hitching her diaphanous dress –
these were the words she cried out in bitter finality,
cheeks tearfully reddened, sobbing wretchedly:

'Is that all there is, cynic, entice me from home,
abandon me to this god-forsaken shore, Theseus?
Stealing away, forgetful of deities,
off home, smuggling the freight of broken promises?
Not one idea flipped your mind from such a heartless
conclusion? You found no deeper emotions
to draw from your stony heart, show me no finer feelings?
What a far cry from the smooth-talking, sweet-sounding

blandishments, or false expectation you led me
to believe of perfect weddings, a blissful marriage –
all these the winds toss about, atomised nothings.
From now on no woman should trust a man's promise,
nor hope that what a man says is a sign of truth.
As long as their hearts lust after controlling you
there's nothing they dare not pledge, no promise reserved,
the moment his needy desires satiated
he becomes forgetful, vows far less important.
But it was me who dragged you free of the maelstrom
when you tripped, preferring to substitute my brother
than lose you, the deceiver, at the point of crisis.
The price of this for me, a cadaver picked at
by animals and birds with no peace in the earth.
What lioness birthed you behind a desolate
rock, what ocean threw you clear of the waves' pull,
what Syrtis, what lethal Scylla, what Charybdis,
that you throw away life's spoils realised thus?
If marriage to me fell short of your designs
on account of a father's old-fashioned values –
in spite of all of this – you could have shipped me home
as your slave-girl to toil for you out of total love,
massaging your feet in mineral water,
folding crimson coverlets over divans.

'So why should I cry out beyond my wits in pain
vainly to the uncaring heavens, indifferent
to listening, or responding blankly to my cries –
he, instead, will be halfway home at this minute
without a living being in sight of this coast.
So Fortune, entirely indifferent to my need,
refuses me an audience to hear my sad tale.
All-ruling Jupiter, would that in the first place the
Cecropian armada not reached Cnossos,
nor, handing the dreadful man-beast doomed gifts,
that lying captain harboured his vessel at Crete,
nor, with malicious intent beneath honeyed smiles,
*he* had enjoyed our hospitality as a guest!

Hopelessly lost, what can I hold to, discarded?
Should I toil up Ida's peaks? A vast chasm
expands between: the water is wide as treacherous.
Dare I expect my father's aid? He I abandoned,
favouring my brother's blood-soaked boy assassin?
Be content with devotions of my husband,
who eludes me, oars flexing against the ocean?
Instead this isolated beach, deserted rock,
the surrounding oceans offer no sea-lane off,
no route to leave by, hopeless, all is soundless,
all desolation, all this signifies the end.
But death will not darken the light behind my eyes,
and before feeling exits my fatigued body,
before that, betrayed as I am, I demand recompense,
requiring finally, complete, heaven-sent justice.

  'Thus you, whose vengeance echoes men's darker actions,
Eumenides, crowned with serpents writhing,
exhaling diabolic fury, boiling over –
I demand your audience, to hear a just case,
which I, unfortunate waif, wrench from the heart
doomed with no choice but pursue blinded with anger,
as these troubles are my truthfully heartfelt offspring,
my heart's labour; do not let my cries be lost, let
go; instead, just as Theseus left me all alone
in such a state of mind, oh deities, leave him with his.'

  After she laid bare herself with such a torrent of words,
demanding revenge, the extreme penalty,
the Heavenly Power nodded unstoppable
approval, so that the earth moved, the seas boiled over,
the universe violently shook galaxies.
But Theseus, his thoughts impenetrable with darkness,
dropped all advice for forgetfulness,
which until then totally focused his attention,
forgetting to haul high the right sign for his pensive
father, telegraph his safe sighting Erechtheus.

At the beginning, the story goes, son about to sail free
of the goddess's citadel, Aegeus,
kissing his heir whispered directions:
'Boy, my only boy, dearer to me than my years
whom I am required to dispatch on a questionable
journey, recently returned to me at the end
of my days, because my fate and your hot bravery
wrench you away against my judgment – my fading
vision not yet satisfied with seeing your face –
I will not wish you on your way with a fond farewell
nor permit you run up signals of a windward fate,
instead, first, export the discomfort of my heart
smearing my white locks and grey beard with earth and dirt
then drape your departing mast with dark-dyed sails
so my deep sadness and smouldering disquiet
be flagged as Iberian iron-blue.
On condition she who lives on Itonus, who
guaranteed to save us and Erechtheus's land,
will permit you bathe your right hand in the bull's blood,
please see to it these instructions I lay in your mind
stay strong and true, not forgotten with time's passing,
in order that as your quick eyes set sights on home
lowering mourning signs, dark-dyed sailcloth,
you raise, untwisted brilliant-white spinnakers,
so that as soon as possible I witness the signs,
great happiness for me at your joyful return.'

These directions, to begin with, were the first things
on Theseus's mind, but in time were as clouds drifting,
then storm-blasted from snowy-peaked mountains.
And so the father, scanning the horizon above
the battlements, his eyes swollen and red from the tears,
momentarily glimpsed the shadow of a blooming
sail, stepped out from the most precipitous cliff,
understanding Theseus obliterated by Fate.
And so, entering a home grieving for his father
headstrong Theseus had to face up to the same

damage of forgetting that caused Minos's daughter pain.
Simultaneously, she gazed on a vanishing dot,
replaying countless heartfelt labyrinthine scenes.

From another place on the coverlet Iacchus,
his group of Sileni Nysa and Satyrs
attending, lustful, flew to you, Ariadne.

* * * * * * * * * * * *

Fanatical Thyades whirled around the god,
head tossing declared Bacchic 'euhoe, euhoe',
some waved thyrsi with concealed points above their heads,
some play about with hacked-up body parts of the bull,
others, wrap-around snakes coiling themselves,
others processed, carrying *orgia*, in boxes
none of the uninitiated should know about,
high-held hands tapping drumbeats rhythmically,
or tinny cymbals rattling noises out of their bronze,
multitudes blowing their bass-drone racket,
shrieking piccolos scraping melodies away.

These great characters decorated epically
this coverlet enfolding the divan.
When the young people of Thessaly were happy
they had seen it all, they moved aside for the gods,
resembled Zephyrus troubling a flattened sea,
the daybreak breezes swelling sea-surges,
whilst Aurora breaks before the onward-moving sun,
so beginning softly, urged by the lightest wind –
processing, shattered with bubbling laughter –
the wind becoming stronger, increase on increase,
peak and crest further away in sparkling light –
so, departing through the palace's front porch
the visitors burst out, each one rushing home.
And so, with them completely dispersed, first Chiron
from Pelion's mountain-tops carrying country
offerings: all the flora of Thessaly's groves
from across the region, or beside the river's flow
cultivated in Favonius's temperate warmth,

these he presented bound together, unsorted;
soothed by the heady scents the palace swooned and smiled.
Immediately, Penios arrived from Tempe,
Tempe, that enclave surrounded by thickest woods
celebrated by Haemonian Dryads dancing,
not unladen: he handed on, roots whole and intact,
massive beeches and high laurels with straight trunks,
alongside these offerings, the bending poplar trees burnt
Phaeton's sibling, and flexing cypresses.
All the walls about the palace woven with his screen
that the vestibule be festooned in greenery.
Next in line after him, creative Prometheus,
scar-tissue faintly showing of long-ago
tariffs settled, shackled hand and foot to flinty rock
dangling above oblivion from craggy
overhangs, then the Father of Gods appeared
from on high, accompanied by wife and children, leaving
Phoebus, his sister, Idanus's mountain-dweller: –
you and your sister alike treated Peleus
with contempt, and she snubbed the wedding of Thetis.

Once they had found their places in straight-backed ivory chairs,
the dining tables were dressed with assorted dishes,
then, at the same time, bodies rattling with old age,
Parcae (a threesome) recited prophesy.
Brilliant white gowns wrapped all about their shivering bodies,
falling groundward ankle-length and crimson-trimmed,
rose-coloured garlands decorated their dazzling white hair,
manipulated busily their infinite work.
The left hand grips the spindle wrapped around in wool,
the right hand nimbly teasing the fibres down, shaping
with fingers turned upward, then twisting down with the thumb,
spinning spindles around circular flywheels,
and then all the time biting and straightening the thread,
wool fibres adhere, puckering dried-up lips
that before had roughened the now slick and supple thread.
Under their feet, safely stacked, the shimmering balls of wool,
tidied away, wicker baskets overflowing.

As they played each strand in turn, voiced with clarity
divine hymns in prophetic melodies –
hymnals no epoch to come will prove false or untrue:

'You, with inherited distinction exceed bravery,
mainstay of Emanthia, dearest offspring
to Ops, listen to the Sisterhood's prophesy
on this special day, the true source, destiny's sequence:
    *quickly running spindles weave complexity.*

'At last, he who grants a groom his desires will arrive,
Hesperus, this brilliant star will escort a wife
who will overcome your heart with love's tidal wave,
happily indulging your conjugal slumbers,
encircling arms smoothly embracing necks.
    *Quickly running spindles weave complexity.*

'No palace has sheltered a love as strong as this,
no lovemaking has enjoined lovers so deeply
as that binding Peleus and Thetis today.
    *Quickly running spindles weave complexity.*

'A boy-child unknowing fear, Achilles,
will be born, not showing the enemy his back,
but a brave chest, frequently winning long-distance
races against the trail-blazing roe.
    *Quickly running spindles weave complexity.*

'None of the heroes will prove his match face-to-face,
Phrygian badlands flooded with Teucrian blood
during the interminable Trojan siege,
falling to Pelops's third-generation descendant.
    *Quickly running spindles weave complexity.*

'His unparalleled adventures and brilliant
feats, mothers will retell at their sons' burials
as they pull down their untidy hair from snow-white crowns,

tearing wrinkled breasts, fists quivering.
*Quickly running spindles weave complexity.*

'Like the cropper who slices as he advances,
dense wheat ripening in yellow fields under hot sun, he
wields menacing steel levelling Trojans.
*Quickly running spindles weave complexity.*

'Witness to his valiant deeds, Scamander's flow
flooding the Hellespont via every
artery, diverting with mounds of the butchered dead,
heating the conduit with carcasses.
*Quickly running spindles weave complexity.*

'Finally see he will be repaid hereafter
when his circular grave in the raised tumulus houses
the sacrificed virgin's deathly white limbs.
*Quickly running spindles weave complexity.*

'Then as Fate decreed the battle-fatigued Achaeans
energy to sever Neptune's enchanted
shackles, freeing the Dardanian city,
his raised grave was flooded by Polyxena's blood, axed
knees buckled, a sacrifice, headless.
*Quickly running spindles weave complexity.*

'Forward then, indulge the lovemaking long expected,
bridegroom embrace the goddess happily,
and have the bride handed on to her keen husband.
*Quickly running spindles weave complexity.*

'Her nurse returning early the following daybreak,
realises yesterday's necklace no longer
fits, nor need her mother fret over a daughter tricky
or estranged, but imagine grandchildren.
*Quickly running spindles weave complexity.*'

The Parcae declared divinations long
ago for Peleus, heartfelt prophesies.
In centuries past deities would physically
appear, visiting the righteous homes of leaders,
before religious beliefs were rejected.
Regularly the Father of Gods from his spangled
shrine would observe one hundred bulls axed in ritual
sacrifice, his day of celebration.
Regularly, roaming Liber urged before him
raving Thyades, off Parnassus, hair
wild, as Delphians hurried away from their city
happily welcoming him, altars smouldering.
Regularly, in the thick of battle, Mavors,
or quick-footed Triton's consort, or the young girl
of Amarynthus appeared, cheering on the ranks.
But once the globe was polluted by criminal acts
mortals driving just causes from envious minds,
brothers steeped in brotherly bloodletting,
sons failing to commemorate parents,
fathers praying for sons' funerals
to experience the delights of the virgin-bride,
a godless mother sleeping with her innocent son
sins without fear and defies the holy Penates –
so by mixing good and bad in devilish chaos
we forfeited the deities' tolerances.
Thus they never descend to our celebrations,
nor tolerate direct contact with broad light of day.

*Book Three*

## 65

Although I'm utterly drained by grief, Hortalus,
   distracted by despair from the know-all Virgins,
my mind's eye birthing still more stillborns for the Muses,
   vision wobbly to a vanishing-point –
not long since a wave rose on the full flood of Lethe
   to lap my brother's death-white foot,
snatched from my view, buried in a Trojan ditch,
   then crushed beneath the beach at Rhoetum

\* \* \* \* \* \* \* \* \* \* \*

   sentenced never to gaze on your face? Who
I love more than life itself with a capital 'L',
   evermore sing sad songs for your dying,
just as the Daulian pipes between bough and shades,
   mourning Itylus she laments murdering –
still, in the face of such deep sorrow, Hortalus,
   I will mail you these fine lines of the son
of Battus, so you'll know your requests weren't scattered
   to the four winds, forgotten by yours truly,
just like an apple dispatched (registered) as a sign
   by her lover, drops 'plop' from a girl's lap,
hid in the dress's folds covering her bosom,
   simultaneously as her mother
enters the bedroom, bumping all along the floor,
   as a ruddy flush blooms across both girl's cheeks.

# 66

He who observed the pin-prick lights of Infinity,
    who combed the stars for risings and settings,
how the sun's fire and punishing heat is eclipsed,
    how stars click round skies through the fixed phases,
how Trivia was relegated to Latmus,
    dear love enticing her from her orbit –
he was Conon: spotted me at the sky's doorway
    curls from Berenice's hairstyling,
shimmering brilliantly, she'd variously
    offered the gods lifting her arms to pray,
at the moment the king emboldened by marriage
    set out to pillage the Syrian lands,
sporting the dear traces of the night's encounter
    he'd fought to cast off the clothes of a virgin.
Do newly wedded brides loathe Venus? Or do they
    upset parents' joy with crocodile tears,
blubbering at the threshold of the marriage suite?
    The gods as my witness, they are liars.
I understood this to be the case from my queen's
    continued anguish as her king went to war,
and, so you say, was left behind and grieving not
    for a marriage bed, but a lost brother.
How to the very depths sadness ravaged your soul!
    Your heart utterly inconsolable,
such derangement of the senses, drained of sense! Yet
    even as a bright young thing you were brave.
Do you misremember the bold action, which saw
    you royally married, who braver dared?
But what a send-off for your man, such sad goodbyes!
    God, how many times you rubbed tears away!
Which powerful god transformed you? Or perhaps lovers
    cannot stand the absence of beloveds?
With that you promised me to all gods, spilt some bull's
    blood too, sealing your cherished husband's

safe homecoming. In short order he'd totted up
  the vanquished Asia against Egypt's border.
With these conquests, I am offered up to the gods
  as pledged, a fresh sacrifice to old honour.
Grudgingly, O queen I was parted from your scalp,
  grudgingly, I vouch by you and your crown,
he who takes this vow in vain will reap what he sows.
  Who would choose a face-off against drawn steel?
Even that great peak was eclipsed, there was none greater
  the glittering seed of Thia ascend,
as the Medes cut a fresh channel, as the young
  savages' flotilla glided through Athos.
What is a curl to do when peaks fail to steel?
  Jupiter, wipe out the entire Chalybes,
and he who first mined the earth for iron deposits,
  who discovered the technique for wrought iron.
Cut: that very minute my sister curls were weeping
  over my loss, when the twin brother of
Ethiopian Memnon showed, stretching his wings.
  The winged horse of Locrian Arsinoe
wafts me to heaven, flitting through the darkest night
  to rest in the purest lap of Venus.
For this task, Grecian immigrant of Canopus,
  Zephyritis, seconded her envoy;
and then, speckled about the star-spangled cosmos,
  apart from Ariadne's gold tiara,
affixed above, I might take my shining place,
  platinum blonde, devoted offering;
drenched with spray on course to the houses of the gods,
  the goddess raised me, morning star with the old.
Brushing the pinprick lights of Virgo and raging
  Leo, nearby Callisto, Lycaon's child,
I click into my place, heading languid Bootes,
  who drops, dips last minute, merged with the Deep.
Despite the gods tramping over me through the night
  I'm restored by break of day to Tethys –
with your permission, Rhamnusian girl, allow

me to say, without dread of truth-telling,
not if the stars shred me with malicious whispers,
    simply unlock what is stored in my heart –
I take little pleasure, tormented apart
    parted forever from my queen's coiffure;
formerly, as a virgin, she abstained wifely
    scents, while I imbibed countless low-priced unguents.
So you, who waited for that long-desired morning,
    do not give up your bodies to loving
partners untying your bodice, laying your bosom bare,
    until the onyx pot offers me up
heady scents – *your* onyx upholding a true bed.
    But girls who surrender themselves to grubby
adultery, ah, make sure their offerings are dried out:
    I demand no spoils from the immoral.
But instead, you brides, forever grant peace and calm,
    forever lasting love live in your house.
O queen, when tracing the map of constellations,
    paying homage to Venus on holy days,
don't allow your lady-in-waiting go without
    scents, instead shower me with endless gifts.
Damnation to the stars! I would be a royal curl,
    Orion shimmer beside Aquarius!

## 67

Oh, treasured by married men, treasured by parents,
    hello, and might Jove himself keep you well,
front door, word is you served Balbus generously
    at the time when the old chap was in charge,
yet rumour is you did for his son wretchedly,
    the old boy gone, and you the bride's threshold.
Go on, spill the beans, why does the street say you changed,
    shirked off your vows to your elderly owner.

'This is not – with your permission Caecilius,
    my present master – my fault, which they claim,
nor can they allege I've committed immoral acts,
    even if local gossip says so –
because whenever something dodgy crops up
    all together people shout: "Door's to blame!"'

One simple contradiction is no substitute,
    everyone must know, be helped to face facts.

'But how? When no one enquires or takes the trouble.'

    Do tell, and don't hold back on the detail.

'First things first, the tale I was handed a virgin,
    that's lies. Her last husband hadn't laid a finger;
his dagger dressed to the left, a pendulous root,
    never pressed his shirt about the midriff.
Yet word has it the father beat about the bed
    of his son and defiled the household.
Either his flaming lusts had clouded his judgment,
    or the son was impotent and sterile,
and by other means more sinuous were devised
    techniques to peel the girl's tights and pants off.'

You tell us what a fine, faithful father he was,
    one who pisses in his own son's lap!

'But that's not the only thing Brixia knows of,
    overshadowed by Cygnus's lookout post,
the town by which slides the Mella, golden, softly,
    Brixia, loved mother of my Verona,
reports Postumius and Cornelius's love-games,
    with whom the girl was crudely adulterous.
At this one is bound to say, 'Door how do you *know*,
    your permanent post your master's entrance,
unable to tune into the locals, and lodged
    below the lintel, swung open, then shut?'
Frequently I've overheard her and faint voices
    of slave-girls chatting about her vices,
naming names I've named, obviously not thinking
    through I might possess either ears or tongue.
And, she touched on one I'd best keep quiet about
    by name, he might just arch his ginger brows –
a tall chap once caught out by a major court case,
    a made-up birth, a belly full of lies.'

# 68a

The fact you are hard-pressed by the Fates and bad luck,
 dispatch this little missive smudged with tears –
a man wracked by storms whipped up on an ocean swell,
 crying out for assistance at death's door,
on whom sacred Venus confers no tranquil sleep,
 exiled to a cold and lonely bed;
nor do the Muses hold much delight in fine verses
 of the Ancients, your insomniac mind
twitching – most satisfying this: you name me friend –
 request delights of the Muses *and* Venus.
But you may not be aware of my difficulties,
 Manlius, concluding I spurn friendship:
I want you to know I have slipped beneath Fate's
 inundation, there'll be no gifts from me.
With that first day I donned the manly white toga
 as my prime awakened to joyous spring,
I acted the lover; no stranger to the Lady
 mixing care with bittersweet love potions,
but my pursuit of *that* is lost to my brother's
 death, totally. Oh, brother torn from me,
you, yes you brother, obliterated my spring,
 our entire inheritance alongside.
Alongside you every good thing of mine has died,
 good things buoyed up by your love while you lived.
Since he went I've entirely expunged from my mind
 every superficial thought or pastime.
You write to tell me what a shame Catullus is
 in Verona where the top-drawer elite
rub arms and legs to keep warm a lonely bed
 which, Manlius, is not a shame, just sad.
Excuse me my failure that I cannot offer
 you the delights sorrow cheated of me.
Now, I don't have a great library of learned writings
 to call on – I'm based in Rome: that's my home,

that is my place, where I live my life to the full,
    just the one trunk of books joins me up here.
As this is the situation I don't want you
    concluding I'm grudging or too tight
to fulfil either of your demands, had I means,
    I would volunteer, unsolicited.

# 68b

Muses, I cannot fall dumb about Allius,
   his aid and the charity of that aid,
in case the passage of time and its obscurity
   cover with blinding night that charity,
so I insist in telling, you must spread the word,
   ensure these sheets declaim down the Ages,
\* \* \* \* \* \* \* \* \* \* \* \* \* \*
   posthumous, his reputation increased,
permit no spider work her thread out of the air
   to obliterate Allius's lost name.
You are aware of the sadness the duplicity
   of the goddess Amathus heaped on me,
scolded, smouldering as the Trinacrian rock,
   or the Malian fount below Oeta
at Thermopylae, my red eyes constantly sore
   with crying, my cheeks dowsed in showery rain,
similarly, as from the mountain tops gleaming,
   a brook shoots across green-weeded pebbles
to plunge vertical through precipitous gullies,
   over a busily populated
thoroughfare, supplying refreshment to passers-by
   when the baking heat cracks up ploughed fields,
or just as are seamen buffeted by black squalls
   find a softer leeward breeze intercedes,
reply to their pleadings of Castor, of Pollux –
   this was Allius, this was his charity.
To a gated estate with private road he gave
   me access, a house (and mistress of that house),
under whose eaves together we shared our lovemaking.
   Here my blinding vision with silent footsteps
rested her dazzling foot a moment on the worn-
   smooth doorstep, tilts forward sandal squeaking,
as long ago, consuming love for her groom drew
   Laodamia to Protesilaus's

house, a house half-built for want of blood-sacrifice
    to satiate gods of the firmament.
I desire for nothing, Rhamnusian virgin,
    without reason and the gods' permission!
How so the hungry altars demand sacrifice
    of the true, Laodamia understood,
husband lost, he bodily torn from her embrace
    after a first and before a second
winter of dark nights relieved her unquenched ardour,
    so she might survive a shattered marriage,
that the Parcae were well aware was not far off
    the second he bore arms against Troy's walls.
At that moment, Helen's rape, Troy turned back upon
    herself the fury of the Argive leaders,
Troy (the horror!) Europe and Asia's sepulchre
    Troy, putrid remains of men and heroic
Deeds, which visited on my brother lamentable
    death? Oh brother ripped from me in my sorrow
oh brother the pleasure of broad daylight buried,
    our entire inheritance alongside.
Alongside you every good thing of mine has died
    good things buoyed up by your love while you lived,
You now distant, not surrounded by family
    headstones, or close-by ancestral remains
but laid out at decadent Troy, terrible Troy
    lost to a remote field, in exile's ground.
To that city the elite flowering of Greece
    raced, abandoned their home-fires, kith and kin,
so Paris may not take delight in the mistress
    he seized, easy, leisured, abed, at length.
Which is why, most beautiful Laodamia,
    something more precious to you than life itself
was torn away – your husband, the riptide of desire
    dragging you under, down the dark void
as the Greeks speak of, close-by Cyllenean Pheneus
    the marshland is transformed to fertile earth,
the alleged son of Amphitryon, once upon
    a time reportedly pierced the mountain

core as he nailed the Stymphalian vultures on
　　straight arrows, ordered by a lesser master,
so the doorstep of paradise was stepped across
　　by one new god, nor Hebe stay unwedded.
But your adoration ran deeper than that void,
　　trained your innocence to carry the burden.
Not so precious to the man nearly out of time
　　is the unexpected heir his daughter
cradles, a boy at long last, matched to inheritance,
　　a name inscribed to sign and seal the will
and wipe the smiles from predatory relatives,
　　scares off the bird of prey hovering overhead.
Never did a dove take pleasure in her blinding
　　lover, although hearsay says she collects
kisses outrageously – peck, peck pecking away –
　　more ardently than lascivious women.
But on your own you overtook this passionate
　　excess when you came to your white-haired husband
my dearest gave over little or not at all
　　dazzling as she slid into my embrace;
and Amor darting around here and darting there
　　radiant and blinding in saffron robes.
Not satiated solely by one Catullus,
　　we can tolerate the odd regression –
she's discreet – in case I seem fussy or silly:
　　for even Juno, the highest on high,
swallows her fury over her husband's weakness,
　　on hearing of Jove's endless love antics.
It is inappropriate to pit gods and men

　　　*　*　*　*　*　*　*　*　*　*　*

*　*　*　*　*　*　*　*　*　*　*

　　stop this unappealing fuss of a father.
Indeed, she was not handed me by her father
　　in a house sweet-smelling of the Orient,
but no the marvels she stole that enchanted
　　for me, pilfered from her husband's boudoir
this, adequate sufficiency on condition

she makes note the occasion with a white stone.
This offering, all my best effort, made of poetry,
    Allius, repays your generosity,
protects your family name against long-term decay
    today, tomorrow and day after day,
to this the gods will stack up more offerings just as
    Themis rewarded those in the Golden Age.
May you and your lady be contented with Life
    and the villa where we once cavorted,
and he who matched us * * * * * * *
    who, in my case, was the good beginning,
particularly she more than all the rest, dearest
    shining planet whose life makes mine worth living.

# 69

No cause for you to ponder why no lady's keen,
    Rufus, to tangle her legs about yours,
Although you wear her down with the choicest of skirts
    and the delicacy of lucent jewels.
What's undone you is the hot gossip all about:
    a smart goat lingers, stinking out your pits.
This concerns all – hardly surprising – bestial,
    which no decent woman would bed down with.
Either fumigate this olfactory pandemic,
    or don't ponder why the ladies escape.

# 70

My woman would marry none, so she says, other
    than me, not if Jupiter pressed his case.
Declares: – what a woman pledges a keen suitor
    is better scripted for air and quick streams.

# 71

If the goat-stink of the pits rightly afflicted one,
    or crippling gout justified agony,
Your competitor who's messing with your girlfriend
    has perfectly fused your complaints to a tee:
Each session he does the business he beats the pair –
    the stink torments her, the gout murders him.

# 72

Once Catullus was the only one who knew you,
    Lesbia, you'd not hold Jove before me.
I delighted in you not simply as a man
    and 'friend', but as a man with his family.
I have found you out: despite my blazing desires
    you're far too trashy, and more vacuous.
'How can I know?' you inquire. Reinforcing such
    a wrong, lovers lust more but are less fond.

73

Give up the expectations, waiting on 'thank yous'
    from someone, or that he can show friendship.
The ungracious are everywhere. Good deeds don't count –
    *au contraire* – they are a drag and dangerous.
Experience tells me, whom no one has bullied
    more than him; *that* one, my latest 'best friend'.

# 74

Gellius was aware of his uncle's stern words
  at hand-holding or smutty innuendo.
To evade these himself he 'kneaded' uncle's wife,
  flipping uncle into Harpocrates.
He gained his just desserts: now, if he crams uncle's
  mouth, the uncle will be stuffed full for words.

# 75

Lesbia, my mind plumbed low via your weakness,
    obliterated with its own duty,
neither caring for you, even though you're the best,
    nor ceasing to adore you whatever's next.

# 76

If, to recollect all the past good things he's done,
    a man realises pleasure in friendship;
His covenants unbroken, nor in a cabal
    used the good words of gods to exploit men,
Then, stored in the many years ahead, Catullus,
    numerous good times laboured from spurned love.
For what honourable deeds can be said to be done
    to anybody, all you did and said.
In total these squandered on ungracious love,
    why then prolong your agony further?
Why not be strong of mind, retreat from where you are,
    defeat unhappiness gods overthrow?
It's tough to sever longstanding love finally,
    it's tough, someway you need to achieve this,
This your last throw of the dice, battle to glory,
    this has to be your aim, able or not.
Oh gods, if you can find pity, if you offered
    relief to one in their final moments,
Gaze on my agonies, if my life resembles
    purity rip out this mortal affliction,
Which seeps insinuating poison through my veins
    to expel all joy from my heart's depths.
I look no more she reciprocate my feelings,
    or, beyond hope, she desire chastity.
I hope for wellbeing, purged of this malady,
    oh gods, allow me this for my service.

## 77

Rufus, my assumed *compadre*, trusted vainly –
    vainly? No indeed: my debt my ruin.
This the way you seeped in, eating out my vitals.
    Ah! Tearing out of me all the good things,
Tearing out, ah, viciously toxic to my life,
    deathly infection of the friends we were.

# 78

Gallus has brothers, who are hitched to a smart wife
    for one, with a smart son for the other.
Gallus the pretty man organises a tryst,
    so the pretty girl beds the pretty boy.
Gallus the simple man, blind to his own marriage:
    uncle lectures on uncle's adultery.

# 78b

But what gets my back up is how your stinking phlegm
    has pissed on the virgin lips of a virgin.
You won't walk away with impunity. Across
    Time celebrity will broadcast your name.

# 79

Lesbius is a beauty. Not true? Lesbia
    wants him more than you, Catullus, and your whole
Line; the 'beauty' auctions Catullus and his line,
    if he gains three kisses through acquaintance.

## 80

What explanation, Gellius, how your ruby lips
    reflect more whiteness than winter snowfall
When you arise at crack of dawn, or the eighth
    hour awakes you from long afternoon slumber?
There's something in the offing: is the gossip true
    that you gorge on the male member's wholeness?
Why of course. The busted balls of sad Victor shriek
    out loud, and your milky, sodden goatie.

# 81

Of all the crowd is there not one, Juventius,
   a beautiful man, to whom you could forge
An attachment besides that stranger from dead-end
   Pisaurum, more washed out than a flea-bitten
Statue, who you love for now, who you elevate
   above us, and you blindfolded to the error?

# 82

Quintius, you'd have Catullus owe you his eyes,
  Or one thing as valuable as eyes.
Don't extirpate what is far more significant
  Than eyes, far more valuable than his eyes.

# 83

Lesbia abuses me before her husband,
  which pleases the bloody dimwit no end.
Indifferent arse. If forgetting me she were mute
  she'd be fancy-free: instead her cursing
And spitting means I nag her thoughts – more important
  she's furious. She's on fire, has to chatter.

# 84

He says 'haspirations' when negotiating
    aspirations, and 'hinsinuations'
Meaning insinuations – Arrius speaking
    'hinsinuations' with true conviction.
I understand his mother, his freedman uncle
    and his mother's parents spoke that way.
Then he was stationed in Syria, resting ears,
    hearing those very words properly spoken
With no haunting worries over their missed sayings –
    without warning the horrible rumour:
The Ionian Sea, as Arrius stepped off
    the boat, not Ionian – Hionian.

# 85

I loathe and I love. You maybe want to ask why.
    I can't tell. It's under my skin and I'm wracked.

## 86

Most think Quintia the best. She's fresh-faced, six foot,
    upright. I'd concur on these details,
The ultimate looker – never. There's nothing sexy
    to her straight back, nothing saucy or hot.
Lesbia's the best, she's the one, completely stunning,
    stealing Venus's looks from everyone.

# 87

Not one lady can claim she's honestly adored
    as my Lesbia was adored by me.
No promise was ever so firm as that written
    in the knot, by my adoring of you.

## 88

What's happening, Gellius, when a man plays around
    with stepmother and sister, *au naturel*?
What's happening, he won't permit uncle be a spouse?
    You realise how gross an outrage that is?
So gross an outrage, Gellius, distant Tethys,
    nor Oceanus, sire to Nymphs, can wash clean,
For what could be grosser, how much lower could he reach?
    Not an inch, even if he sucked his own cock.

# 89

Gellius is slight. Definitely. Mother so
   giving, so healthy, sister so frisky,
An uncle so giving, the family a world
   full of girls, no wonder he's a beanpole.
Even though he lays a hand on what he shouldn't,
   there're these many good grounds for his slightness.

## 90

A magus, offspring of Gellius's damnable
    intercourse with his mother – learns Persian spells:
A magus is the issue of mother and son,
    if wicked Persian belief tells the truth,
So their seed with pleasing song pays homage to gods
    as the omentum reduces in fire.

# 91

I expected, Gellius, your fidelity,
    on this awful, this doomed love we have shared,
Not through close friendship or dependability,
    or your skills to avoid thinking lewd thoughts,
But it was obvious she I had this 'big love'
    for, was neither your mother nor sister.
Despite intimate and longstanding acquaintance
    I couldn't accept *that* your driving force.
You believed it so. What misdemeanours bring you
    joy, which hint at evil villainy.

## 92

Lesbia is constant in her abuse of me,
    chatters away. I'll die if Lesbia
Loves me not. What signs? The feelings are mutual,
    I abuse her – die if I love her not.

# 93

I'm not much interested, Caesar, placating you,
  nor bothered which side you're batting for.

94

Nob of Knobs fucks. Fucking nob of knobs? That's for sure
the saying goes: if the root fits, pot it.

# 95

*Zmyrna*, my dearest Cinna's, issued nine summers
and nine winters since she was his first thought!
For his part Hortensius five hundred thousand
   * * * * * * * * * * * * * * *
*Zmyrna* will run quickly via Satrachi's waves;
grey-templed generations read *Zmyrna*.
Volusius's *Annals* will perish close by Padua,
gift wrapping mackerel for many a year
Close to my heart this little masterwork . . .
let the plebs hail verbose Antimachus.

## 96

If the soundless mausoleum can welcome good
    and precious offerings in our anguish,
Calvus, from the desire through which we set aflame
    past love, and cry for friends long abandoned,
Certainly, Quintilia suffers less sadness
    at her life cut short, than joy from your love.

# 97

I supposed (God give me strength) there be no difference
    I breathe in Aemilius's gob or dirt-box,
The one being no fresher to the fetid other,
    truth is the dirt-box is germless, gentler –
Toothless. The gob has gnashers eighteen inches long
    and gums worn out as a knackered shit wagon.
And there's more: where it gapes open broad as the vag
    of a mule which pisses the summer's heat.
And he's fucking all the fillies, turns on the charm,
    the grindstone's where he belongs, with the ass.
Any girl touching him might kiss the shit-box of
    a hangman, running with diarrhoea.

## 98

Of all people, putrid Victius, the charge can
  be levelled at you of vacuous chatter.
With that tongue you might, had you had half an excuse,
  kiss the dirt-boxes and the farmers' boots.
If you desire the undoing of us completely,
  Victius, speak up, you'll win outright.

# 99

Honey-lipped Juventius, as you teased away,
  mine, a kiss, sweet as sweet ambrosia.
Not without reparation: for an hour and more
  I suffered the very worst of tortures,
Time told me, as I sought forgiveness, you unmoved by
  my crying, your fury unabated.
At that very moment, you doused your lips with water,
  and rubbed them hard with delicate fingers
To make sure you contracted nothing from my mouth,
  as it were from a call-girl's pissy gob.
You were happy to quickly pass me to Love, outcast,
  for unimaginable crucifixion.
The little kiss transmuted from ambrosia
  into bitter as bitter hellebore.
This the price exacted for a miserable lover,
  no more kisses shall I pinch of yours.

## 100

Caelius desperate for Aufillenus, Quintus
   for Aufillena, buds of Verona,
This one for the brother, that one for the sister:
   'brotherly love' as the saying has it.
Who should I bet on? Caelius, your comradeship
   invaluable, proof through fiery trials,
As yesterday's inferno engulfed my very core.
   Caelius, be lucky, conquer in love!

# 101

Toiling via numerous lands, over countless
    seas, I arrive, brother, with this last offering,
Final tokens which the dead carry with them,
    and mouth sayings above your mute remains
Hopelessly, as Fate stole away your living presence,
    my sad brother, heartlessly torn from me.
In any case, please accept these tokens I offer,
    as are handed over to those passed on.
Completely devastated with a brother's crying,
    to the end, brother, 'ave atque vale'.

# 102

If an honest comrade trusted a confidence
    to one whose fealty was not in doubt,
You will discover me of that faith, Cornelius,
    tight-lipped, transformed into Harpocrates.

# 103

Please hand back the ten thousand sesterces, Silo,
    then be hot and ugly as you choose,
Or if the cash gives you the kick, then don't come on
    the pimp, bullying and loutish to boot.

## 104

Do you credit me with the damning of my life,
   who is as valuable as my eyes?
Never, if I would, would my love be so extreme –
   you and Tappo make it up, out of air.

# 105

Nob of Knobs attempts to mount the peak of Pipla:
the Muses fork him off the tops. Down, down.

## 106

When you see a lovely lad accompany an
   auctioneer, one infers he'd auction himself.

# 107

If a thing ever occurred, ever so wanted
    to who'd dared not dream – such delightful thoughts.
So this delight purer than gold to the both of us,
    Lesbia, you return to me wanting.
My wanting you returned I'd not dared to dream by
    your free will. Oh, daylight lighter than light!
Who could be so lucky in love as this, who's to say
    there's more good one could want from life, who?

## 108

If, Cominius, now that you are old and grey,
    the mob terminated your dissolute life,
Without question, first to go the tongue, enemy
    to virtue, thrown to the guzzling vultures;
Eyes popped out for ravens to suck down their black throats,
    innards for dog food, and the wolves what's left.

## 109

You hint, dearest, our love shared equally for two
    might prove a lasting ecstasy – forever?
Good gods, if only her vows were possibly true,
    she declares sincerely, body and soul,
so let us continue, forge ahead a shared life,
    an infinite treaty between friends.

## 110

Aufillena, decent call-girls are well reviewed
    and fairly paid for services rendered.
You tricked me out of your bond, treated me badly,
    wrong, you take, take, take, refusing to give,
A well-born girl is honest in deed, not to offer
    is chastity, Aufillena, but you
Claw in the presents, withhold services, worse than
    a hoarding whore, turning any trick for trade.

# 111

Aufillena, for a wife to be happily
   co-habiting with a husband is best,
But it's fair enough to bed every man instead
   of mothering brothers via her father.

## 112

You're a man for all men, Naso, not many men
   follow, Naso, man for all men – and gay.

## 113

In Pompey's first consulship, Cinna, there were two
   did 'business' with Maecilia: he's consul
Again, the two are constant, a thousand grown up
   with each one. How generous adultery.

## 114

Nob of Knobs is wealthy by all accounts at Firmum,
  possessing many, many wondrous things –
all the wildfowls, fish, arable, meadow, and game.
  Good for nothing: expenditure outstrips means.
I don't care that he's filthy rich, if he's caught short.
  Celebrate his land, so long as he's skint.

# 115

Nob of Knobs holds nearly thirty acres of meadow,
  forty of arable; the leftovers marsh.
How can he fall short outstripping Croesus for wealth,
  where this farmland possesses wondrous things,
meadow, arable, vast forests, endless wastelands
  to the Hyperboreans, Oceanus?
Every magnificence, the largest yet, he himself –
  no man but the scariest Nob of Knobs.

# 116

Often with learnèd and straining thoughts I have tried
    conjuring some lines of Battiades
To bring you round, that you desist in your attempts
    to ceaselessly aim arrows at my head.
But now it is clear my work was wasted effort,
    Gellius, my appeals without foundation.
The shower of your projectiles I'll sidestep:
    to your cost you'll be wounded by mine.

# Glossary of Names and Places

Names are followed by the number(s) of the poem(s) in which they appear.

**Achaea/n** (64). *The Greeks fighting the Trojans.*

**Achilles** (64). *Son of Peleus and Thetis, greatest of Greek heroes of the Trojan Wars.*

**Acme** (45). *Unknown.*

**Adonis** (29). *Beautiful youth adored by Venus.*

**Adriatic, Hadria** (4, 36). *Sea between Italy to the west and the Balkan states to the east.*

**Aeetes** (64). *King of mythical status. Holder of the Golden Fleece.*

**Aegeus** (64). *Theseus's father, and suicide.*

**Aemilius** (97). *Unknown.*

**Aganippe** (61). *Sacred spring on Mount Helicon, a place of inspiration.*

**Alfenus** (30). *Sometime friend of Catullus, with humble origins.*

**Amarynthus** (64). *One of the Nereids.*

**Amastris** (4). *Town similar to Cytorus.*

**Amathus** (36, 68b). *Also known as Cyprus. Venus was worshipped here.*

**Ameana** (41). *Unknown woman of high birth fallen on hard times, or courtesan.*

**Amphitrite** (64). *A Nereid, from the sea.*

**Amphitryon** (68b). *Married to Alcmene, and father of their son Iphicles.*

**Ancona** (36). *Sheltered harbour town on the Adriatic. Associated with the cult of Venus.*

**Androgeos** (64). *Son of Minos, murdered by Aegeus.*

**Antimachus** (95). *Poet of the sixth century, ranked second to Homer.*

**Antius** (44). Unknown.

**Aonia** (61). Another name for Boeotia.

**Aquarius** (66). *Sign of the zodiac.*

**Aquinus** (14). *Annalist, poetaster and fool, otherwise unknown.*

**Argive, Argos** (64, 68b). *Refers to the crew of the ship, Argos, but also the city on the south Peloponnese.*

**Ariadne** (64, 66). *Daughter of Minos and Pasiphae. Abandoned by Theseus, rescued by Bacchus.*

**Arrius** (84). *Windbag, orator.*

**Arsinoe** (66). *Wife of Ptolemy II. Mother-in-law to Berenice.*

**Asinius Marrucinus** (12). *Dinner guest and napkin thief.*

**Asinius Pollio** (12). *Younger, (more talented?) brother of napkin thief.*

**Athos, Mount** (66). *A peninsula extending into the Aegean, with a mountain at its end.*

**Attis** (63). *A youthful enthusiast for the cult of mother-goddess Cybele, who castrates himself in an act of devotion he comes to regret.*

**Aufillena/us** (100, 110, 111). *Brother and sister, otherwise unknown.*

**Aurelius** (11, 15, 16, 21). *Friend of Catullus, friend of Furius.*

**Aurora** (64). *Dawn.*

**Aurunculeia, Junia** (61). *Bride of Manlius Torquatus.*

**Balbus** (67). *Of Verona, otherwise unknown.*

**Battiades** (116). *First king of Cyrene. Hellenic poet Callimachus was thought* *to descend from him.*

**Battus** (7, 65). *King who built Cyrene.*

**Berenice** (66). *Wife of Ptolemy III. After leaving a lock of her hair at the shrine at Zephyrium to ensure the safe return of her husband from battle in Syria, it was discovered again as a new constellation, Coma Berenices.*

**Bithynia** (10, 25, 31). *Rich province in western Asia Minor, and a posting for Catullus.*

**Bononia** (59). *Military base, otherwise unknown.*

**Bootes** (66). *Constellation including Arcturus.*

**Brixia** (67). *Close by Lake Garda, and in the foothills of the Alps.*

**Callisto** (66). *Hunted with Artemis; pregnant by Zeus; transformed into a bear; elevated from real bear into the Firmament as the Great Bear.*

**Cecrops** (64). *One of the first (and mythical) kings of Attica.*

**Caecilius (I)** (35). *Unknown friend of Catullus.*

**Caecilius (II)** (67). *Unknown Veronese property owner.*

**Caelius Rufus** (58, 69, 77, 100). *Caelius and Rufus are very likely the same person. Follower of Cicero, who defended him during the Cataline conspiracy. Sometime lover of Clodia. Also possibly the subject of 71, 73.*

**Caesar, Julius** (11, 57, 93). *Soldier, statesman, demagogue, and friend of Catullus's father.*

**Caesius** (14). *Unknown, verse dabbler.*

**Calvus, Licinius** (14, 50, 53, 96). *Poet and close friend of Catullus. Acquaintance of Cicero.*

**Camerius** (55, 58b). *Unknown.*

**Campus Minor** (55). *A particular but unidentified Campus in Rome.*

**Canopus** (66). *Port at the mouth of the Nile.*

**Castor** (4, 37, 68b). *Twin brother of Pollux, both protectors of seaman and sea-passengers.*

**Cato** (56). *Freeman, poet. Died in penury of old age.*

**Chalybes** (66). *Inhabitants of Asia Minor.*

**Charybdis** (64). *A whirlpool off the coast of Sicily.*

**Chiron** (64). *Grandfather of Peleus and teacher of Achilles. A Centaur.*

**Cieros** (64). *Town in Thessaly.*

**Cinna** (10, 95, 113). *Close friend of Catullus and one of the 'Neoteric' group of poets. He went to Bithynia with Catullus.*

**Circus Maximus** (55). *Near the Forum in Rome.*

**Cnidus** (36). *Town on the peninsula of Cos, associated with the cult of Venus.*

**Cnossos** (64). *City of Minos, home to the Labyrinth and the Minotaur.*

**Colchis** (64). *Mountain at the eastern extreme of the Black Sea, the location of the Golden Fleece.*

**Colonia** (17). *Small town adjacent to Verona.*

**Cominius** (108). *Unknown.*

**Conon** (66). *Astronomer and friend of Archimedes, c. third century BCE.*

**Cornelius (Nepos)** (1, 102). *Friend of Catullus, and writer of a three-volume history of the World.*

**Cornelius (ii)** (67). *Unknown adulterer.*

**Cornificius** (38). *One of the 'new' poets or Neoterics, and confidant of Catullus. Fought and died for the Senate.*

**Crannon** (64). *A Thessalian town.*

**Crete** (58b, 64). *The biggest island in the Aegean Sea.*

Croesus (115). *A king of huge wealth, c. 550 BCE.*

Cupid(s) (3, 13, 36, 45). *Son of Venus, causing passion (and pain) among the victims of his love-tipped arrows.*

Cybele, Cybebe (63). *Mother goddess, the Magna Mater. Her followers carried out ecstatic rituals, which the authorities had to curb. In Rome her temple was located on the Palatine, adjacent to Clodia Metelli's house.*

Cycladic (4). *Islands in the middle of the Aegean Sea.*

Cygnea/us (67). *Fort overlooking Brixia.*

Cyllene/an (68b). *Town and mountain in Arcadia.*

Cyrene (7). *Large coastal city west of Libya.*

Cytorus (4). *Town on the shores of the Black Sea, with the surrounding lands supplying wood for boat building.*

Dardanians (64). *Trojans.*

Daulian (65). *On the old road from Orchomenos to Delphi.*

Delian, Delos (34). *Small island in the Cyclades, probably Diana's birthplace.*

Delphians (64). *The place of the Delphic Oracle, and navel of the World.*

Dia (64). *Site of Ariadne's abandonment by Theseus, a small island off the north coast of Crete. Later Naxos and Dia became the same place.*

Diana (34). *Goddess of hunting and the moon.*

Dindymos (35, 63). *A mountain in Phrygia, and centre for the worship of Cybele.*

Dione (56). *Mother of Venus.*

Dryads (64). *Tree nymphs, usually in the vicinity of oak trees.*

Dyrrachium (36). *Harbour town on the Illyrian coast.*

**Egnatius** (37, 39). *Unknown love rival.*

**Emathia** (64). *Same as Thessaly.*

**Eous** (62). *The Dawn.*

**Erechtheus** (64). *One of the first kings of Athens.*

**Erycina** (64). *Another name for Venus.*

**Etruria, Etruscan** (39). *One of the most important early peoples of Rome, their lands were northwest of Rome.*

**Eumenides** (64). *A trio of goddesses, the Furies.*

**Eurotas** (64). *A river passing through Sparta, eventually reaching the Aegean.*

**Fabullus** (12, 13, 28, 47). *One of Catullus's firmest friends, but otherwise unknown.*

**Falernian** (27). *A type of wine cultivated close by the Appian Way.*

**Favonius** (64). *A goddess of the winds.*

**Fescennine** (61). *Ribald verses reserved for processing weddings through the streets.*

**Firmum** (114). *South of Ancona close by the Adriatic coast.*

**Flavius** (6). *Unknown.*

**Formiae** (41, 43, 57). *Bustling town on the coast and near the Appian Way.*

**Fufidius** (54). *Friend of Cicero, mocked by Horace as dubious money lender.*

**Furius** (11, 16, 23, 26). *Poet and friend of Catullus. Friend of Aurelius.*

**Gallae** (63). *Eunuchs in the service of Cybele.*

**Gallus** (78). *Unknown.*

**Gellius** (74, 80, 88, 89, 90, 91, 116). *Another lover of Clodia Metelli, and* *sometime friend or acquaintance of Catullus.*

**Golgi** (36, 64). *Town in Cyprus, and centre for the veneration of Venus.*

**Gortynia** (64). *Region of Greece in the Peloponnese.*

**Haemonia** (64). *Alternative name for Thessaly.*

**Hamadryades** (61). *Woods nymphs, physically embodied as trees.*

**Harpocrates** (74, 102). *Egyptian god of silence.*

**Hebe** (68b). *Goddess of eternal youth and Hercules's wife after his ascent to the gods.*

**Helen** (68b). *Of Troy, wife of Menelaus, King of Sparta. Her kidnap by Paris sparked the Trojan War.*

**Helicon** (61). *Mountains in Boeotia, hang-out for Muses and Hymen.*

**Hellespont** (64). *The Dardanelles.*

**Hercules** (38, 55). *Mightiest of mortals, and Argonaut.*

**Hesperus** (62, 64). *The Evening Star.*

**Hortensius Hortalus** (65, 95). *Lawyer, sometime poet, friend of Cicero.*

**Hurricane Sebastian** (25). *Cross reference to Frank O'Hara's poem 'Having a Coke with You', to pick out the cultural equivalence of Late Republican Rome and mid-twentieth-century New York as centres of cultural influence and tolerance of sexual difference.*

**Hymen** (61, 62). *God of marriage, living on Mount Helicon with the Muses.*

**Hyperboreans** (115). *A mythical race beyond the land of the north winds.*

**Hyrcania** (11). *A faraway country to the East.*

**Iacchus** (64). *Alternative name for Bacchus.*

**Ida, Mount** (63, 64). *A mountain south of Troy, as well the name of a mountain located on Crete.*

**Idalium** (36, 61, 64). *Town in Cyprus, with cults devoted to Venus, Jupiter and Aphrodite.*

**Ionian Sea** (84). *Water between Greece and Italy.*

**Juno** (68b). *Wife of Jupiter.*

**Juno Lucina** (34). *Cult absorbed into the worship of Juno.*

**Jupiter, Jove** (4, 7, 34, 55, 66, 67, 68b, 70, 72). *Roman deity equivalent to the Greeks' Zeus, father and leader of the gods.*

**Juventius, Juventii** (24, 48, 81, 99). *Young man Catullus is very fond of, otherwise unknown.*

**Ladas** (58b). *Spartan Olympian runner, who ran so fast he left no footprints.*

**Lanuvium, Lanuvian** (39). *Ancient city of Latium, located just off the Appian Way.*

**Laodamia** (68b). *Wife to Protesilaus, unable to bear his death as the first to set foot on the shore at Troy.*

**Larian shores** (35). *Lake Como.*

**Larissa** (64). *Town in Thessaly.*

**Latmos, Mount** (66). *A mountain where Endymion was kissed asleep by Diana.*

**Latona** (34). *Mother of Diana.*

**Leo** (66). *Sign of the zodiac beyond Virgo, beyond Berenice's Lock.*

**Lesbia** (5, 43, 51, 58, 72, 75, 79, 83, 86, 87, 92, 107). *Most likely (but not definitely) Clodia Metelli, a highborn woman ten years older than Catullus, and the subject of most of his love poems addressed to women. She is supposed to have poisoned her husband and had many lovers. Poems not addressed to her directly, but which are probably about her: 2, 3, 7, 8, 11, 36, 68b, 70, 76, 85, 91, 104, 109.*

**Lethe** (65). *A river of the Underworld.*

**Libo** (54). *Unknown supporter of Caesar.*

**Libya** (7, 45, 60). *The coastal region of northern Africa.*

**Liguria** (17). *Land on the coast of northern Italy.*

**Locris, Locrian** (66). *A region of central Greece.*

**Luna** (34). *Reflected light.*

**Lycaon** (66). *King of Arcadia, father of Callisto.*

**Lydian** (31). *A people believed to be of eastern origin.*

**Maecilia** (113). *Unknown adulterer.*

**Maenads** (63). *Female followers of Dionysus, but interchangeable as a term for fanatics following Cybele.*

**Malians** (68b). *Northern Greek tribe.*

**Manlius Torquatus, Allius** (61, 68a, 68b). *Friend of Hortensius and underling of Cicero, from an old aristocratic family that served on the Senatorial side in the Civil Wars.*

**Marcus Tullius** (49). *Cicero.*

**Marmurra** (29, 57). *Engineer in chief to Julius Caesar and close confidant. Alleged sexual libertine and allegedly corrupt. A big spender. Other poems possibly referring to him are: 41, 94, 105, 114, 115.*

**Mavos, Mars** (64). *God of War.*

**Medes** (66). *A land southwest of the Caspian Sea.*

**Mella** (67). *River close by Brixia.*

**Memmius** (28). *Governor of Bithynia (57 BCE), Catullus was on his staff, not a great success for the poet.*

**Memnon** (66). *King of Ethiopia.*

**Menenius** (59). *Husband of Rufa, otherwise unknown.*

**Midas** (24). *King of Phrygia, and mythical figure, who turned everything he touched into gold.*

**Minos** (64). *King of Crete.*

**Naso** (112). *Unknown.*

**Nemesis** (50). *Goddess and vengeful pursuer of sinners and those that do wrong.*

**Neptune** (31, 64). *Roman god of seas and rivers.*

**Nereids** (64). *Nymphs from the Aegean.*

**Nicaea** (46). *A city in Bithynia.*

**Nonius** (52). *Unknown.*

**Novum Comum** (35). *Town on the foothills of the Alps, north of Milan.*

**Nymphs** (88). *Mainly water-bound female goddesses, but also frequenters of caves, trees and grottoes.*

**Nysa** (64). *Origin of Dionysus, possibly as far away as India.*

**Oceanus** (64, 88, 115). *A river encircling the earth, spouse of Tethys.*

**Oeta** (68b). *Greek mountain.*

**Oetaean** (62). *Alternative to the word Hesperus.*

**Olympus** (62). *Where the gods reside.*

**Ops** (64). *Goddess of fertility and spouse of Saturn.*

**Orcus** (3). *God of the Underworld, the Underworld itself.*

**Orion** (66). *Killed by Artemis, cast into space as a constellation.*

**Otho** (54). *Unknown. May have worked for Caesar.*

**Padua** (95). *Northeastern Italian town.*

**Parcae** (64, 68b). *The Fates and weavers of Man's future.*

**Parnassus** (64). *Home to Dionysus and the Maenads.*

**Parthians** (11). *Famous in the period for mounted soldiering as cavalry and archers.*

**Pasithea** (63). *A Grace, wife of Hypnos (Sleep).*

**Pegasus** (58b). *Winged horse born of the blood of Medusa, who was beheaded by Perseus.*

**Peleus** (64). *A lucky Argonaut, whose prize was the goddess Thetis as wife.*

**Pelion, Mount** (64). *A mountain located in Thessaly.*

**Pelops** (64). *Father of Atreus, husband of Hippodamia.*

**Penates** (64). *Household gods.*

**Penelope** (61). *Faithful and patient wife of Odysseus.*

**Penios** (64). *River and god.*

**Perseus** (58b). *Son of Jupiter and Danae, he killed the Medusa aided by the gift of Mercury's winged sandals.*

**Persia** (90). *Territory covering large part of the known East, eventually annexed by Alexander the Great.*

**Phaeton** (64). *Son of Apollo big-headed enough to drive his father's chariot before falling into the River Po.*

**Pharsalus** (64). *A town in Thessaly.*

**Phasis** (64). *River, whose course flows through Colchis to the Black Sea.*

**Pheneus** (68b). *Town in Arcadia, below Mount Cyllene.*

**Phoebus** (64). *Same as Apollo.*

**Phrygia/n** (46, 61, 63, 64). *Area of Asia Minor and parts of Bithynia, also another name for Trojan.*

**Phthiotis** (64). *Northern borderlands of Thessaly.*

**Pipla** (105). *A spring dedicated to the Muses.*

**Piraeus** (64). *Natural port just outside Athens.*

**Piso** (28, 47). *Contemporary of Cicero, possibly Julius Caesar's father-in-law.*

**Pollux** (37, 68b). *Castor's twin. As a pair they are the Dioscuri. Pugilist.*

**Polyxena** (64). *Sacrificed as an offering by Priam for Achilles' death, to be his bride in the Underworld.*

**Pompey** (113). *General and politician, rival and, eventually, son-in-law to Caesar.*

**Pontus/ic** (4, 29). *The Black Sea and parts of the surrounding coast including Bulgaria and Romania.*

**Porcius** (47). *Unknown.*

**Postumia/us** (27, 67). *Probably brother and sister, but otherwise unknown.*

**Priapus** (47). *God of gardens and lust. Usually identified as having a large phallus.*

**Prometheus** (64). *Stole fire (free will) and gave it to Mankind. Chained to rock for thirty years for his pains by Jupiter with an eagle eating his liver until released by Hercules.*

**Propontis** (4). *Sea between Dardanelles and the Black Sea.*

**Protesilaus** (68b). *First Greek ashore at Troy, and first to die. Husband of Laodamia.*

**Quintia** (86). *Unknown.*

**Quintilia** (96). *Wife to Calvus.*

**Quintius** (82, 100). *Unknown.*

**Ravidius** (40). *Unknown love rival.*

**Remus** (28, 58). *One of the mythical brothers and founders of Rome.*

**Rhamnusia/n** (66, 68b). *Same as Nemesis, same as Fate.*

**Rhesus** (58b). *Thracian king of myth, whose fast horses were acquired by Odysseus and Diomedes.*

**Rhodes** (4). *Large island in the southeast of the Aegean Sea.*

**Rhoeteum** (65). *Meaning Trojan.*

**Romulus** (28, 29, 34, 49). *One of the mythical brothers and founders of Rome.*

**Rufa, Rufulus** (59). *Sister and brother (?), unknown.*

**Rusticus** (54). *Unknown.*

**Sabine** (39, 44). *A region near Tibur, but not fashionable. The people had a reputation for toughness.*

**Sacae** (11). *Nomads wandering in the region now known as Tashkent.*

**Saetabis** (12). *Famous for its Spanish linen.*

**Salisubsalian** (17). *Otherwise unknown local deity to the town of Colonia.*

**Sappho** (35). *Greek lyric poet of the seventh century BCE, who lived on Lesbos. Poem 51 is Catullus's translation of her Fragment 31.*

**Satrachus** (95). *River in Cyprus. Meeting place for Adonis and Aphrodite.*

**Saturnalia** (14). *Midwinter celebration. Roman version of Christmas.*

**Satyrs** (64). *Hooved and horned followers of Dionysus.*

**Scamander, River** (64). *River running from Mount Ida to the Hellespont.*

**Scylla** (60, 64). *Twelve-headed monster waiting for sailors opposite the whirlpool of Charybdis.*

**Septimius** (45). *Unknown.*

**Serapis** (10). *A deity imported from Egypt, worshipped by women as a cure for sterility.*

**Sestius** (44). *Politician and friend of Cicero's.*

**Sileni** (64). *Similar to satyrs.*

**Silo** (103). *Unknown.*

**Simonides** (38). *Greek poet, 556–467 BCE.*

**Sirmio** (31). *Rocky outcrop extending into Lake Garda where Catullus's family owned a villa.*

**Socration** (47). *Unknown.*

**Stymphalus/ian** (68b). *Town in Arcadia, with lake infested by man-eating birds.*

**Suffenus** (14, 22). *Unknown.*

**Sulla** (14). *Unknown.*

**Syria** (6, 45, 66, 84). *Land on eastern Mediterranean seaboard, the Euphrates to the east and Arabian desert to the south. One of the richer regions of the Republic in this period.*

**Syrtes** (64). *Shallow and treacherous water off what is now Libya and Tunisia.*

**Tagus, River** (29). *River flowing through Spain and Portugal, entering the Atlantic to the south of present-day Lisbon.*

**Talassius** (61). *Roman for Hymen.*

**Tappo** (104). *Unknown.*

**Taurus, Mount** (64). *A leafy mountain in Asia Minor.*

**Telemachus** (61). *Son of Odysseus and Penelope.*

**Tethys** (64, 66, 88). *Goddess of the sea, daughter of Heaven and Earth.*

**Teucer, Teucrian** (64). *Trojan whose forebears were kings of Troy.*

**Thallus** (25). *Young, gay man, otherwise unknown.*

**Themis** (68b). *Goddess of Justice and mother of the Parcae.*

**Thermopylae** (68b). *The pass from north to south of Greece.*

**Thespia/n** (61). *Town in Boeotia.*

**Thessaly** (64). *Eastern and central Greece.*

**Theseus** (64). *Son of Aegeus, killed the Minotaur, eloped with Ariadne, leaving her on Naxos (Dia). Neglecting to raise the white sail, his father threw himself from the cliffs as Theseus returned from his travels.*

**Thetis** (64). *Nymph, goddess and wife of Peleus. Mother of Achilles.*

**Thia** (66). *Same as Macedonia.*

**Thracian** (4). *Area east from Macedonia, including Bulgaria, parts of modern-day Turkey and eastern Greece.*

**Thyades** (64). *Alternative to Maenads and first followers of Dionysus.*

**Thynia** (31). *Town situated in Bithynia.*

**Thyone/ian** (27). *Also known as Semele, mother of Bacchus.*

**Tibur/tine** (39, 44). *Today's Tivoli. Fashionable in the Late Republic as the Hamptons were for New Yorkers in the 1950s and 1960s.*

**Transpadene** (39). *North of the Po River. Where Catullus's family was supposed to have come from.*

**Trinacrian** (68b). *Of Sicily.*

**Triton** (64). *Marine god and son of Poseidon and Amphitrite.*

**Trivia** (34, 66). *Another name for Diana, here connected to the idea of crossroads and the Underworld.*

**Troy, Trojan** (64, 65, 68b). *The far northwest of Asia Minor, close by the Dardanelles, and the setting for the Trojan Wars.*

**Umbria/n** (39). *Region of central Italy, north of Rome.*

**Urania** (61). *One of the nine Muses, and mother of Hymenaeus.*

**Urii** (36). *Place of veneration for Venus, now unknown.*

**Varus** (10, 22). *Friend of Catullus.*

**Vatinius** (14, 52, 53). *Unappealing social and political climber, whose behaviour landed him in the courts on several occasions.*

**Vibennius** (33). *Unknown frequenter of public baths.*

**Venus** (3, 13, 36, 45, 55, 61, 62, 66, 68a, 86). *Roman goddess of Love and physical passions. Mother of Cupid, mistress of Mars.*

**Veranius** (9, 12, 28, 47). *Close friend of Catullus and Fabullus.*

**Verona** (67, 68a, 100). *Catullus's birthplace, close to Lake Garda.*

**Victius** (98). *Unknown.*

**Victor** (80). *Connoisseur of oral sex, otherwise unknown.*

**Virgo** (66). *Sign of the zodiac, to the left of Berenice's Lock in the Firmament.*

**Volusius** (36, 95). *Unknown amateur and windbag.*

**Zephrion, Zephyritis** (66). *Outcrop of land at the meeting of the Nile with the Mediterranean.*

**Zephyrus** (64). *The West Wind.*

**Zmyrna** (95). *Epyllion penned by Cinna.*

# Acknowledgements

I thank the following editors, where some of these translations first appeared: *Fire, fragmente, Free Verse: a Journal of Contemporary Poetry and Poetics, PN Review, Poetry Review, Poetry Wales, Snow, Stand,* and *Vanitas.* I thank also Kelvin Corcoran and Ian Davidson for publishing *Twenty-Five Carmina* at Gratton Street Irregulars, and Alec Newman for publishing *Carmen LXIV* at Knives Forks and Spoons.

I also want to thank all the people who work at Hawthornden Castle, where I completed my version of 'Poem 64' as part of a residency there in 2009. I want to thank the authors with whom I spent my time during July of that year at breakfast and dinner, and about the grounds of Hawthornden, walking and in conversation.

Special thanks go to Michael Schmidt for all his enthusiasm and encouragement over the years. I completed this manuscript as a PhD under his supervision at the University of Glasgow.